The Dory Model Book

The
Dory
Model
Book

A WOODENBOAT BOOK BY HAROLD "DYNAMITE" PAYSON

Design by Richard Gorski
Printed in the United States of America
Cover photograph of Dynamite by Sherry Streeter,
of models by Ken Woisard
All other photographs by the author

Plan of 14-foot Higgins and Gifford Banks dory, Chapter 3,
drawn by Howard I. Chapelle, courtesy of
W.W. Norton, 500 5th Avenue, New York, NY 10036

All other plans courtesy of Robert Lane, Friendship, Maine

A WoodenBoat Book

ISBN 0-937822-45-0

Dedication

*This is dedicated to all boat modelers:
past, present, and future.*

Acknowledgements

My thanks go to:

*My wife, Amy, for her patience
in typing the manuscript.*

Bob Lane, boatbuilder, draftsman, and friend.

*Peter H. Spectre, editor and friend, who got me
started in this project and then had to
make sense of it all before it could see print.*

*Jay Hanna, master modeler, who, when I complained
that everything I built for a model seemed to come out
oversized in scale, told me to cut apart the plans
and use them for patterns.*

CONTENTS

Introduction

INTRODUCTION

Every so often I go on a construction binge. I'll make something, and like it, and make another, and like that, too, so I'll make a bunch more. Soon I'll be overloaded. Whatever I have been making will take up half the shop and then some. A few years ago, for example, I went on a smelt-bobber binge, and I still have a big box full of the things.

What's a smelt bobber? you ask. It's a float used with a pole-fishing rig for keeping smelt bait off the bottom.

What's a smelt? It's a tiny fish, not much bigger than a largish minnow, that's fun to fish for and, as we say in my stretch of the coast of Maine, is some good eating.

A proper smelt bobber, the type the old-timers used to make, is designed in a way that allows it to lie quietly on the water until the fish hit, then it rises right up and shows you what's going on. The shape of the body and the placement of a dowel in one end are the keys.

One day I needed a proper bobber and went to the store. All they had were those round plastic things with no class at all — the ones that bob in every old direction whether a fish hits it or not. There was nothing to be done but to make my own.

I went all the way with that and devised an efficient production method for knocking them out, one right after another. I even mechanized the painting process (two-tone: white on one half, red on the other). I chucked up the dowel end of the bobber in an electric drill, turned her on, dipped my brush in paint, touched it to the turning bobber, and presto, a perfect paint job and a straight waterline, all in an instant.

I was so pleased with myself that I couldn't stop. I made a box full, perhaps a hundred or so. All I needed was one.

That was it for the smelt bobber building binge, or almost the end (my wife discovered they made excellent Christmas-tree ornaments). That binge was eventually superseded by many more — model airplanes (several hanging from the ridgepole of my shop), sardine carrier models (three, in cases on my workbench), and others — the latest being miniature planked-up dories.

Peter Spectre stopped by the shop a little while ago. With his usual take-it-all-in-one-glance-I'm-in-a-hurry look, he said "Holy Smokes, Dynamite, have you lost your marbles? You've got dories all over the place!"

Pete was referring to the model dories in plain sight, a considerable number by anyone's reckoning. I had a pile more in a box under the bench.

"You want dories, Pete," I said, pulling out the box. "I've got dories." Pete sort of froze there in disbelief, then picked up his little dog Ben, turned around, and walked out the door. I could hear him talking to himself out in

"You want dories, Pete," I said, pulling out the box. "I've got dories."

the yard. Or maybe he was talking to Ben, I don't know. ("He's bonkers. That's all there is to it. He's bonkers.")

The truth is that I had, indeed, gone a little bonkers in the dory department. I had developed a slick method for building the critters and was having a grand old time at it. With the tooling in place I could plank up a dory in 3 hours or so! Before I knew it I had made 30.

So what's so easy about building a model dory?

Visualize a box. That's easy, isn't it? Think plumb and square, and that's easy, too, isn't it? Whether building boats or houses, the concept is basically the same: Visualize a box; think plumb and square.

If it is within your talents to build a simple, rectangular wooden box, with lines squared across it, then you're in business. If you can build this box so that it is reasonably accurate — plumb and square — without any twist, humps, or hollows, you will be in the driver's seat. You will be able to build models of the beautiful dories in this book, and many other models that might come to mind.

Getting started is simple. Building the model, when approached step-by-step, is just as simple. Here, in a nutshell, is what we'll be doing:

■ We will build a solid wooden box.

■ We will put the dory in the box (that is, we will draw the lines of the dory on the outside surface of the box).

■ We will take the boat out of the box (by cutting away the excess wood outside the lines we have drawn).

■ We will now have a plug — an accurate, solid-wood copy of the dory hull — over which we can plank the dory model, and any number of identical dory models we might desire. (See what I mean? In no time at all you can be locked into a dory-model building binge.)

■ On the plug we will temporarily fasten a stem, a transom, and a bottom panel, and then we will commence planking from the bottom to the top.

■ When we reach the top, we will use the top surface of the plug to mark the sheer of the dory, we will transfer some of the lines from the plug to the model, and then we will pull the dory model from the plug.

Nice, huh?

Symmetrical in shape, both sides of the model will have the same amount of flare, the stem and the transom will be plumb, and there will be no twist anywhere. And why not? If our box was plumb and square, and if we drew our lines accurately on it, and if we carved our boat — the plug — out of the box carefully, then anything we build on the plug will have to be symmetrical. Even if our workmanship in planking the dory was crude, the result would still have the proper shape of a dory. And make no mistake about it: A properly shaped dory looks right; an improperly shaped one does not.

Bob Lane, the Down East boatbuilder who drew the plans for the dories in this book, used the same technique for defining the shape of the boats on a piece of paper. With a drawing board and a T-square, he laid out the lines on a grid that he drew plumb and square. Instead of a flat sheet of paper, we will use a three-dimensional block of wood.

The advantage of using a plug to build a model of a dory is that you can bring all the small pieces to the large plug. The hull can be built upside down, and the plug can hold the stem, the transom, the bottom panel, and the several pieces of planking precisely in place during the planking process.

If we were to build a model of a dory the same way full-size dories are built, we would find the job significantly more difficult. We would have to build the model right-side up. We would have to deal with shaping the dory's bottom, setting it up in some way to conform to the hull profile shape, and maintaining that shape while we worked on the rest of the boat. We would have to place the frames on the bottom and hold them there, we would have to plumb the stem and the transom, while keeping track of all those miniature pieces. All the while those miniature pieces will be trying to twist and warp out of shape, and usually they will be successful at it.

Past experience tells me that the only way to go is to make an accurate plug and bring all the little pieces to it. This is the foundation of the entire process.

Since we will be carving the plug from a block of wood made from glued-up laminations, which are very

Here I am in my workshop, having just completed a model of a Banks dory.

stable, the plug will keep its shape indefinitely if it is given reasonable care. Since the plug is not likely to become lost — it makes a handsome display model in its own right — and it can't wear out from use, it can be passed down in your family from generation to generation. Think about it. You can establish your own dory-modelmaking dynasty.

Before you get involved in that, however, let's have a look at how full-sized dories were built.

The construction of each of the models described in this book — the Friendship clam dory, the Banks dory, and the Friendship dory-skiff — is virtually the same. Though there are a few subtle and not-so-subtle variations among them, generally, if you can build one, you can build them all. I have therefore approached the instructions with that in mind. I have devoted most space to the building of the first model, that of the Friendship clam dory, under the assumption that if you build the models in order, you will need less instruction by the time you get to the last. If you decide to build only one model, and it turns out to be the last one in the book, the Friendship dory-skiff, to fully understand how to build it you will have to refer to the instructions for the other models as well. My recommendation is that you read the entire book from the beginning to the end, fix in your mind the general building procedure, then choose the dory you want to model and have at it.

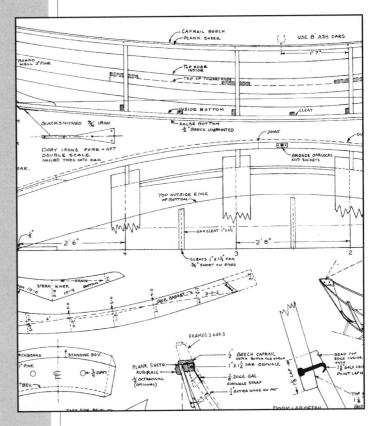

CHAPTER 1

Dory Construction the Old-Fashioned Way

Nobody knows for sure when the first dory was built. John Gardner, in *The Dory Book*, theorizes that it was somewhere around the mid-1700s. Whenever it was, the dory came to be a very popular boat. By the late 19th century, great quantities were being built to supply the growing fishing fleets sailing out of New England and Canadian maritime ports, principally Gloucester, Massachusetts, and Lunenburg, Nova Scotia.

Originally, fishermen handlined for cod and haddock right over the rails of their schooners: a safe and comfortable way to fish, but not the most profitable. Then fishermen discovered that a schooner could launch a fleet of dories on the Banks and, with one man fishing from a dory, cover more territory per man. The result was more fish landed, more pay for the dorymen — who worked under what amounted to a commission system — and greater profits for the owners of the schooners. The further result was a huge demand for dories.

WHY THE DORY?

The design of the dory was ideal for the work demanded of it, and the simple construction of the type allowed economical quantity production. Dories were easy to build and easy to repair, and construction lumber for them, mostly white pine, was cheap and plentiful.

The greatest advantage of the dory for commercial fishing was its seaworthiness, light or loaded with fish. Though the craft was cranky when it was light, it was still seaworthy. A fisherman caught on the Banks away from his schooner in a gale could lie right down in the bottom of his dory and stand a better chance of surviving than if he were in any other type of boat of that time.

Loaded or light, the dory rowed well because of her fine ends. With a load, her crankiness disappeared and she became a stable platform.

A further advantage was that dories were easily carried on the deck of a schooner. Because their thwarts could be removed, several dories could be "nested" — stored upright, one inside another. A nest of anywhere from 4 to 8 dories could be carried on each side of the deck of a typical fishing schooner of the late 19th century, early 20th century.

By the turn of the century, dory building had reached the peak of efficiency. A topnotch team of craftsmen in a commercial dory shop, each man performing a specific job, could build a dory in as little as four hours. This included painting the craft inside and out, usually the same color. The inside painting was the quickest job of all: a can of paint was dumped into the dory and spread around with a mop, then the dory was turned over and the excess paint was allowed to drain out.

I can remember seeing dories being built right-side up in the 1940s and '50s at the Newbert and Wallace boatyard in Thomaston, Maine. I used to go over there to buy lumber for my own boatbuilding. Off to one side of the shop, out of the way of the Eastern-style draggers under construction, Lou Pottle and later Bill Simmons, both of Friendship, Maine, built dories on demand, most as lifeboats for the draggers. Their dragger dories were painted bright orange, inside and out, and were carried upright, fitted with a canvas cover, on top of the pilothouse. Some draggers carried one dory on top of the house, some two.

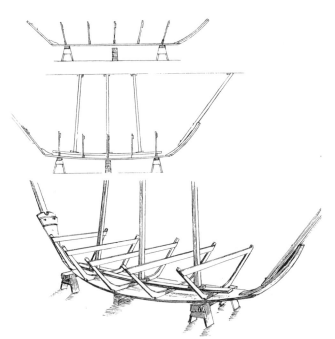

1-1 *The setup for building a traditional Banks-type dory. The proper rocker is obtained by forcing down the bottom with shores braced to an overhead. Drawing by Samuel F. Manning from* The Dory Book, *by John Gardner; courtesy of Mystic Seaport Museum, Mystic, Connecticut.*

HERE'S HOW THEY WERE BUILT

Most dories were built right-side up and by eye, their builders using methods and skills passed on by previous builders. Plans and blueprints weren't used, because they did not exist. Rather, patterns were used for everything and to good advantage. The use of patterns was so universal that while one dory was being finished, a worker was already cutting out parts for the next.

The bottom of the dory was built first. (See Figure 1-1.) It began as 3 or 4 planks laid flat, side edge to side edge, so they would run longitudinally in the boat. These planks were splined and cleated together, and then the entire assembly was sawn to shape. The bottom rocker — the fore-and-aft curve — was obtained by elevating the ends on blocks or short posts and pushing down the middle with a post braced to an overhead joist.

The transom and the stem, both pre-beveled, were positioned at the ends of the bottom, braced to their proper rake, plumbed, and fastened.

Next came the frames, usually sided 1 inch, 5 to a dory. These were positioned on the bottom, spaced the proper distance apart. Cross spalls — temporary sticks — were used to maintain the tops of the frames at the correct distance apart. Ribbands — long battens — were sprung around the sheer on both sides of the boat and fastened to the stem and the transom.

A chalkline was strung from the centerline of the stem to the centerline of the transom. The centerlines of the frames were aligned with this chalkline, and then they were braced plumb and square. Then the boat was ready for planking.

1-2 *My first dory, an old used-up Banks type, at her mooring at Head of the Bay, Owls Head, Maine. The size of the lettering for my name and hailing port is an indication of how proud I was of her.*

The production dory shops had patterns for all the planks, which were lined off with edges that were as straight as possible to minimize the time spent shaping. The garboards went first. They were shaped, beveled, pre-bored for the fastenings, and hung. They were fastened at the chine, the stem, and the transom with blunt galvanized boat nails. Then the rest of the planks were hung, one right after the other, from the garboard to the sheerstrake. Each strake was fastened to the next with smaller galvanized boat nails, which were clenched.

Once the dory had been planked, the gunwales and caprails were installed, and then the thwart risers and thwarts. The holes for the painter were bored through the planking; they were positioned so the painter would snug against the back of the stem rather than bear on the planking. Holes for the stern becket were drilled in the transom, and the becket, which was used for hoisting the dory aboard a schooner, was rigged.

The thole pins were made from ⅞-inch stock, 6 pins per rowing station — two pins and one spare per side.

Many of the dory builders rigged them in a clever way. Holes were bored in the bottom ends and a line looped through them. When rigged for rowing, two pins on a side were in their sockets in the caprail, the line running from the bottom hole in each pin, the third pin hanging in the middle of the loop as a spare. When stowed, all three pins were hanging by the line from the sockets. To get back in business, the doryman pulled down on the spare pin and the two working pins plopped into their sockets in a flash.

A drain hole was bored in the bottom and a tight plug was fitted. On rare occasions a dory would capsize, and to help the doryman stay with his boat until rescued, a becket was rigged to the plug. This was done by boring a hole in the bottom end of the plug and running the becket through it. In use, the becket hung below the bottom of the dory and provided a handhold for the doryman if he found himself in the water. This was a cheap life insurance policy, most likely the only one the doryman had.

DORY DAYS

My own involvement with the dory came when I was just 13 years old. Fiercely independent and wanting to be my own boss, I picked and sold enough blueberries one summer to buy an old used-up Banks dory for five dollars. For another five bucks, I bought ten used lobster pots. I set up my own fishing station at the Head of the Bay in Owls Head, Maine. On the beach, at the high watermark, under an old apple tree, I had a couch, a bait barrel full of free bait (redfish cuttings were free then), pot buoys, toggles, the old traps, and a bunch of other stuff, some useful, some not, gathered from beachcombing. I was in business, my own boss, king of the world, all for ten bucks.

A few years later I was fishing for lobster out of another dory from Metinic Island, five miles to the south'ard of Spruce Head, Maine. One day my dumb cousin was with me. Reaching down, he asked, "What's this for?" and pulled. The geyser of water that hit him smack in the face told him in a hurry. He had pulled the drain plug.

CHAPTER 2

The Friendship
Clam Dory

The first model we will build is the Friendship clam dory, a five-plank round-sided dory from the coast of Maine. This type of dory originated in the town of Friendship, though no one seems to know exactly when. Some sources indicate that the type dates back at least to the time of Wilbur Morse, the famous builder of Friendship sloops, and that Morse built several of these dories for local customers. Later, in the 1940s and '50s, Johnny "Wink" Winkapaw of Friendship built a number of them for local customers; these had a transom cutout for a 5-horsepower outboard motor. Johnny Wink's shop eventually burned down, at which time all his patterns were destroyed, but by then a lot of the dories had been built; some still survive in and around the town of Friendship to this day.

My own interest in the Friendship clam dory came from using one in the late 1940s and early '50s, when I was lobster fishing on the offshore Maine island of Metinic. Fellow lobster fisherman Walter Post, down at the northern end, had one, and I was impressed with its performance.

After leaving the island in 1957, I tried tracking down a Friendship clam dory for my own use, making many trips to Friendship without any success. Later, by a stroke of luck, boatbuilder Bob Lane, owner of Penobscot Boat Works, son of Carl Lane (artist, author, and

2-1 Here's Bob Lane of Friendship, one of the best boatbuilders on the coast of Maine and a man who knows his dories.

illustrator of many books), walked into my shop one day. He said he was from Friendship. My first question to him was, "What about this Friendship clam dory. Can you tell me anything about it?"

Yes, as it turned out, Bob Lane could. Not only that, he could show me one: He had a used-up dory of the type stored on Cranberry Island, off Friendship. After I mentioned that I would like to record the shape on paper for future generations, Bob pulled the boat from its resting place and brought it to a new berth in my dooryard (see Figure 2-1). Bob and I took off the lines, and Bob, being an excellent draftsman, recorded those beautiful lines on a set of plans for full-size boatbuilding or for modelmaking.

Building the model is where I come in. And you, too. Let's do it.

THE PLANS

There are two sheets of plans for building the Friendship clam dory. They are drawn to the scale of 1½ inches = 1 foot, which is an easy scale to work with even if your eyesight isn't top notch. A model built to this scale is 26½ inches overall; that is, from the outside of the stem to the outside of the transom. Plans for building a dory of this size can be purchased directly from me. (You'll find my address and those of companies I'll mention throughout the book in Sources of Supply on page 79).

The plans reproduced here are not to scale. To use them from the book, you can have them enlarged with a photocopier to whatever size you want. For a smaller model than the one described above, you can go to 1 inch = 1 foot, which makes a nice-looking dory 17½ inches overall. The smallest dory model I have made is 6 inches overall, still using the plug method, to fit on the decks of the model sardine carriers *Pauline*, and *William Underwood*.

Sheet One of the plans is for reference. Sheet Two is the one you will spend a lot of time with as a modelmaker, as it contains all the patterns needed to build the model.

Sheet One carries a considerable amount of information, including the profile of the finished dory and a spritsail drawn at ½ inch = 1 foot. At the bottom of the sheet are two scale references you can use if you don't happen to have an architect's scale rule. They automatically match whatever size you increase or decrease your plans to. But I'd buy an architect's scale rule anyway. If you mess with boats and models, you will always be using it.

Pay no attention to the table of offsets or Johnny Wink's bevel board; you won't need them for the model.

Note on Sheet One that Frames 2 and 3 are identical. Note also the construction detail at the top of Frames 2 and 3, which shows the gunwales, the gunwale strap, the rubrails, and the railcap. In addition, note that the false or outer bottom, which on the full-size boat was left square-edged, was made of beech, and was sacrificial (in other words, it was designed to be worn away from dragging the boat off and onto the shore, to be

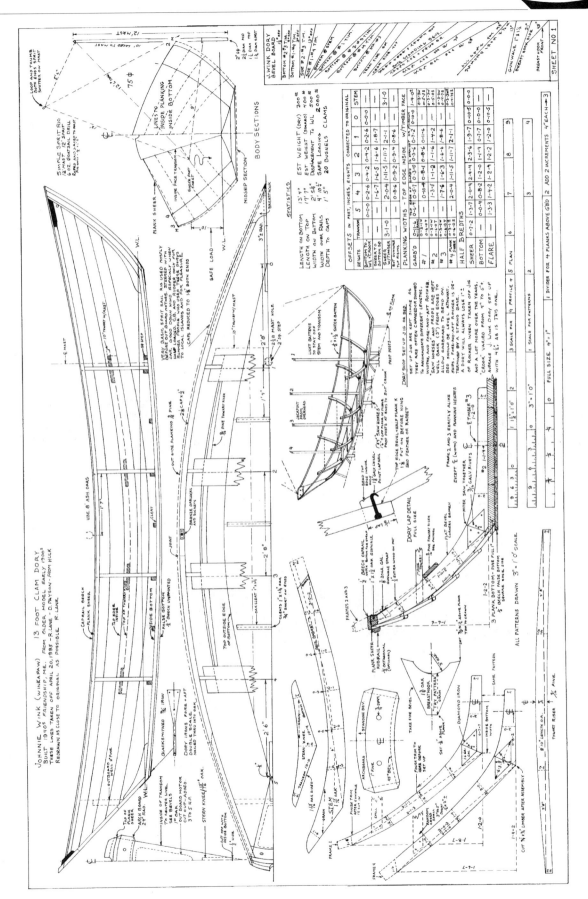

SHEET ONE

replaced as necessary). Keep all these details in mind as you build the model, because including them as drawn will make the result authentic.

Note the body plan on Sheet One, labeled "Body Sections," which on the left side shows the shape of the hull looking forward from aft, and on the right side shows it looking aft from forward as if you had X-ray vision. The dory's lines are drawn to the inside of the planking, which makes building the plug much easier than it would be if the lines were drawn to the outside of the planking. Why? Because the plug itself represents the shape of the dory to the inside of the planking. If the lines were drawn to the outside of the planking, we would have to deduct the thickness of the planking to arrive at the proper dimensions for the plug.

Sheet Two is a modelmaker's dream. Everything is there in pattern form for building a model of the Friendship clam dory, right down to the dory scoop for bailing. All you have to do is cut out these shapes and use them as patterns, which will save you a considerable

amount of time if you want to get right into the woodworking end of things. (Note that Sheet Two does not contain patterns for the block of wood for the plug; that's because the block is a rectangle, and simple dimensions are adequate for building that.) Should you decide to build your model to a different scale, these patterns will still work. Just make the box smaller or larger to fit.

On the other hand, you might want to dispense with patterns and start from scratch, which is what I had to do the first time around. Working with only the information on Sheet One will give you valuable experience that will serve you well when you want to build a model from plans that do not include patterns.

WOOD AND TOOLS
Let's talk briefly about wood and tools before jumping into the building process.

Basswood is my first choice for building a model of the Friendship clam dory and the other dories in this book, because it has fine grain and good finishing qualities

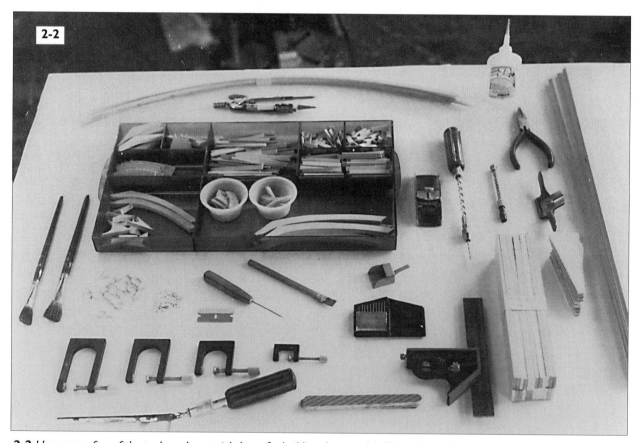

2-2 *Here are a few of the tools and materials I use for building dory models. Those deep-throated modeling clamps are well-nigh indispensable. The box contains various dory parts ready to be fitted. That's a finished dory scoop below the lower right corner of the box.*

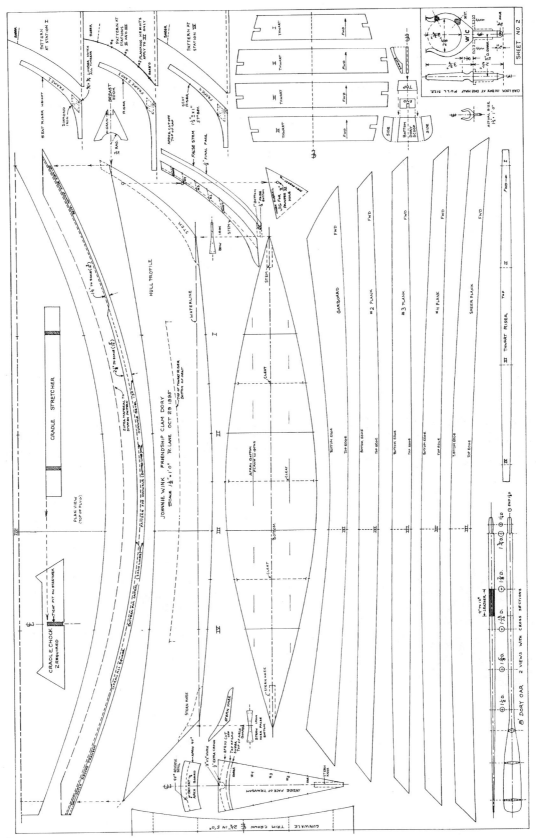

JOHNNIE WINK   FRIENDSHIP CLAM DORY   R. LANE   OCT 29 1995

SCALE 1/2" = 1'-0"

SHEET TWO

whether it is left clear or painted. The cheapest way to buy it is in the rough; you can saw it to size yourself. Generally, rough boards are 1 inch thick or thicker, and can be obtained in almost any length and width you want. At about $2.50 a board foot (1996 prices) this is a bargain when compared to the price of $5.00 for one milled piece ⅜ inch by 4 inches by 2 feet from a mail-order model-supply house. Basswood in the rough can be purchased from hardwood lumber suppliers; I get mine from A. E. Sampson & Son in Warren, Maine.

My second choice for building this model is native Maine white cedar, as it bends easily, and good, clear grain can be found between the knots and the edgings. Pine is my third choice and poplar is my fourth. Pine has its problems: It doesn't carve as easily as basswood, and it is liable to bleed pitch if it is set near a stove to hasten the drying of glue or paint.

There are many other types of wood that will work okay. Perhaps there is a species peculiar to your area that will make excellent models. Before going the mail-order route, see what modelmakers in your neighborhood use and check out what your local lumber supplier has in stock.

For tools, the more you have, the better you can control every aspect of the job and the easier the job becomes. When it comes to large power tools, a table saw, a bandsaw, a scroll saw, and a thickness planer are all right up there on the list headed "Nice to Have." Of the four, the table saw and the bandsaw come first and second.

For small power tools, the Dremel Moto-Tool is mighty handy, with its huge variety of cutters, sanders, and drills designed specifically for it. Add the Dremel drill press attachment to the list of accessories, and you're off to a great start — not that you have to have all this stuff to make a model, but the more you acquire the more independent you become. The happy day might eventually come when you realize that you have all the tools you will ever need to do anything you're capable of doing. I might mention, however, that I have been building full-size boats and models of them for years, and I still run across tools that I know will make some task that much easier if I had one. (See Figures 2-2 and 2-3.)

Tool recommendations, wood recommendations, descriptions of ways of doing things... they're all scattered throughout this book. Take your time. Find a good,

2-3 *More modeling tools, including a number of homemade sanding blocks of various shapes and configurations. The Dremel Moto-Tool at the center, top, has a great number of uses when making small parts.*

comfortable, well-lighted place and read this book through before rushing out to the shop to start milling wood. Sort it all out — the stuff you have, the stuff you want, and the stuff you need — then go to it.

Our first task is to build the plug. Keep in mind that the beauty of the plug isn't important, that the accuracy of it is. Keep your pencils, your tools, and your mind SHARP. Don't be afraid to use your head when something doesn't measure out or look right. My father, who was a carpenter, always told me after I had screwed something up, "Use your head, boy, that's what it's for."

MAKING THE PLUG

The block of wood for making the plug for the Friendship clam dory is 4½ inches high, 8 inches wide, and 27 inches long. It is made from as many pieces of wood as it takes to make a rectangular box of those dimensions. Here's what we will be doing:

■ We will set the slices of wood on edge and glue them so the glue joints will be vertical. We will have, therefore, a block made up of vertical slices, which in naval architect's parlance are known as vertical lifts. The glue lines between the vertical lifts are, in effect, buttock lines — a naval architect's term that sounds mysterious but isn't. I won't go into a long discourse about them, except to say that as you shape the plug they will automatically appear as curved lines in profile; that is, when the plug is viewed from the side.

■ We will use these glue lines to great advantage in carving the plug, because they will indicate as we go whether the plug is symmetrical or not. For example, when these glue lines cross a station line, they should be crossing it at the same height on both sides of the plug. If they cross at a lower point on one side, we can easily see that we have to take more wood off the opposite side of the plug to keep the plug symmetrical.

■ We will designate one of the glue joints as the longitudinal centerline of the pile and hence the centerline of the plug.

Glue Up the Block

If wood of good length for making the plug is in short supply, the outside slices can be pieced out near the ends with no problem, since these areas are cut away when shaping the hull. To make my plug I used 5 pieces of 1⅝-inch thickness and ripped the centerpiece in half to make my glued centerline. But my method isn't written in stone. If you only have ¾-inch stuff around, you can simply increase the number of slices to get the proper width to your block; in that case it will take 11 pieces of ¾-inch stock to get the 8-inch width. For wood 2 inches

thick, you'll need 4 pieces — and so on.

You don't have to be fussy about the type of glue you use for laminating the block. Weldwood dry powder, Elmer's white glue, carpenter's yellow glue (Titebond, etc.), epoxy — they will all do the job.

Glue up the vertical slices of wood on a flat surface, such as the top of your table saw or the kitchen counter if the cook will let you get away with it. Wherever you choose, be sure to lay down wax paper so you won't be gluing your block to the surface.

Keep in mind that the slices, taken together, must be squared-up in cross section. The ends need not be aligned exactly; an approximation is fine. Twist, however, must be rooted out and eliminated, as twist in the glued-up pile means there will be twist in the plug and therefore twist in the finished model.

What about clamps? If your clamps won't open to 8 inches, the width of the block, make your own clamps from ½-inch or thicker plywood sawed with squared openings slightly wider than 8 inches. Glue the slices together, slip two of these clamps over the assembled slices, and drive in wedges just far enough to tighten things up and draw the joints together. (See Figure 2-4.)

Draw the Lines

Draw the station lines on the block after the glue has hardened, but first remove any glue lumps that might interfere with the process. On Sheet 2, Roman numerals mark where the station lines cross the parts of the hull. The distance between these station lines is 4 inches. Square the lines across and around the plug after making sure you have left room enough at each end for the hull. The length of the hull profile pattern is 25⅞ inches; the length of the plug is 27 inches.

2-4 *The glued-up block of wood for the plug. I made the big clamps myself from a couple of pieces of scrap plywood. Clamping power is achieved by driving wedges, as shown.*

Keep in mind that the hull profile pattern, which shows the hull as viewed from the side, is drawn to the inside of the planking — that is, the thickness of the transom, bottom, caprail, and stem cap is not included.

Cut Out the Hull Profile Pattern

From Sheet Two, cut out the hull profile pattern loosely to shape. Do not cut right to the line at this point. Give your roughly cut hull profile a shot of artist's spray glue and stick it to tempered Masonite or $\frac{1}{16}$ inch aircraft plywood, which is available at most hobby shops. Allow the glue to dry for a few minutes, then, with a bandsaw or scroll saw, cut out the pattern precisely to the lines. Lacking either of these tools, a saber saw with a fine-tooth blade will do. Put the pattern in a woodworker's vise, or use clamps to hold it securely. With a strip of sandpaper glued to a flexible batten, sand the edges to fair lines.

What is a fair line? Any curved or straight line that is free from quick humps or hollows is fair. Or, to put it another way, a fair line is a graceful line, straight or curved, that is pleasing to the eye.

Position and Mark the Pattern

With the dory hull profile pattern all nicely faired, we are ready to use it. Lay it on the side of your glued-up block of wood so it is well within the box. Check the position carefully.

When you are satisfied with the positioning of the pattern, measure the distance from the bottom edge of the block to the waterline drawn on the hull profile pattern. Remove the pattern and, with your measurement, mark the waterline around the block of wood, ends and all.

Put the hull profile pattern back on the side of the block, aligning the waterline of the pattern with the waterline on the block, and the station tick marks on the pattern with the station lines on the block. Check that when the pattern is aligned properly it is still inside the box, and if it is, trace around the pattern onto the block. (See Figure 2-5.)

Repeat this on the other side of the block with the pattern turned over, so the bow on each side will be facing in the same direction (check this carefully). In other words, when you are done you will have the hull profile drawn on both sides of the block, aligned with the station lines and waterline. The dory will be in the box plumb and square.

An even more precise way to ensure the exact placement of the hull profile pattern on each side of the block of wood is to use two sliding squares. Position

2-5 *The station lines have been drawn all around the block of wood, the waterline has been established, and the profile pattern has been made and aligned on the block. Now the shape of the profile can be drawn, using the profile pattern as a guide.*

the pattern on the first side of the block as described above and trace around the pattern. Set one square with its body resting on the top of the block, and slide the blade until its end just touches the top of the bow on the hull profile. Set the other square similarly so it just touches the top of the stern. Lock the blades and shift the squares to the other side of the block. Lay the pattern on this side so the station marks on the pattern align with the station lines on the block. Position the top of the bow and the top of the stern so they just touch the ends of the blades on the squares, then trace around the pattern.

Cut and Fair the Sheerline and the Line of the Bottom

With the hull profile of the dory marked on both sides of the plug, now comes cutting time. We are going to take the dory out of the box.

As much as I would love to be able to cut the curves of the sheer and the bottom with a bandsaw, my bandsaw's largest depth of cut is 6 inches and the thickness of the block when aligned for the cut is 8 inches. There are two solutions to this problem: take the work to someone who has a bandsaw with an 8-inch depth of cut, or use the time-honored method.

I use the time-honored method, which is no big problem but does involve a lot of handwork and takes time. Using a handsaw or a portable circular saw, make a series of cuts across the block of wood, from the top down almost to the sheerline and from the bottom up almost to the bottom line. (See Figure 2-6.) Then chip out the excess wood between the sawcuts. (See Figure 2-7.)

Of course, if you have a bandsaw that can make these cuts, then use it. A skip-tooth blade is great for this, and for the rest of the sawing required for the plug. Set the blade to a degree or so off plumb to ensure that the cut will be higher than the sheerline on the unseen underside of the block. You can remove the excess later in the finishing process. If you do not take this precaution, nine times out of ten the cut will wander lower than the sheerline in places, and you will have botched the job. You will then have to laminate pieces onto the block so you can replace the sheerline — a rather embarrassing task not easily done — or worse, start all over again. The latter is

2-6 *The time-honored way of cutting down to the sheerline. It looks ugly, but it works.*

2-7 *Use a hammer and a chisel to chip out the pieces between the saw cuts.*

even more embarrassing. (This also applies to cutting the curve of the bottom.)

Whether you use a bandsaw or the time-honored method, put the block in a woodworking vise and take it all the way to the lines on both sides (sheer and bottom) with a sharp spokeshave and sanding tools. (See Figure 2-8.) If your vise won't open as wide as 8 inches, tack or glue a piece of wood to the block that your vise can accommodate. As always, you are looking for clean, fair lines. When you are done, the block will be concave at

2-8 *Fair down to the sheerline with a spokeshave and a curved-sole sanding block. Check frequently for side-to-side straightness with a ruler or straightedge.*

the topside, representing the sheer of the hull, and convex at the underside, representing the bottom of the hull, and will be flat across.

With the dory profile squared all the way around, including the ends at the bow and the stern (see Figure 2-9), you have done all you can do to ensure that the hull profile is accurate.

At this point, our block of wood looks less like a block and more like a plug, so we will start calling it that.

Establish the Plan View and the Shape of the Bottom

The next step is to reestablish the station lines across the top and the bottom of the plug before we cut the plan view (the top of the plug) and the shape of the bottom. So let's go back to Sheet Two of the plans again.

Note that the pattern for the bottom of the plug, in the middle of Sheet Two, is complete; that is, both sides of the bottom around the centerline are shown. Only one-half of the shape of the top of the plug, the plan view at the top of Sheet Two, is shown. Don't panic. The

2-9 *Because of end-grain, the easiest way to work down to the line at the ends of the block is to use a big woodworker's rasp.*

straight edge indicates the longitudinal centerline; since the hull is symmetrical, you can use the pattern to mark one side of the plan view or top, flip it over, and use it to mark the other side.

Roughly cut out the patterns for the top and the bottom just as you did for the hull profile pattern, leaving a little excess all around. Glue them to Masonite or aircraft plywood, trim the excess, and fair the edges.

Align the centerline of the plan-view pattern with the centerline on the plug's top, and the station lines with the station lines. Note that because the plan view was drawn on flat paper, it needs to stretch a bit to accommodate the curve of the sheer. There's nothing to it. Match the station lines forward, trace around the pattern to amidships, pull the pattern aft to match the station lines aft, and trace around to amidships.

Follow the same procedure in aligning and tracing off the bottom pattern.

Establish the Shape of the Transom

The pattern for the tombstone transom is shown on the left side of Sheet Two. Since the top edge of the transom has a reverse bevel in profile, the length of the transom must be greater on the outside face than the inside to provide enough wood for the bevel. Therefore, add 1/8 inch or more to the length shown, and you won't get into trouble later.

As I have mentioned already, removing excess wood is easy; adding it if you should come up short is not.

There is no need to draw the top of the tombstone shape on the pattern, or the sculling notch (the nearly semicircular cutout shown on the plans). We will do that later after the hull has been planked up.

Position the pattern on the plug, matching its centerline with that of the plug and aligning the pattern's bottom edge so it is flush with the corner of the plug's bottom. When you are satisfied all is right, trace around the pattern.

Cut the Plan View to Shape

When bandsawing the plan view of the plug, we must bear in mind that we are building a model of a round-sided dory. If we cut a straight line from the sheer to the chine, we will remove too much wood and will not be able to create that lovely fullness to the sides. The goal here, then, is twofold: to remove as much wood as possible with the bandsaw and to avoid ruining the shape of the boat by taking off too much, thus making her straight sided.

Examine the body plan of the boat, the view on Sheet One labeled "Body Sections." Note that the frames with the least amount of flare at the top are Frames 2 and 3.

The flare here is about 14 degrees, so set your bandsaw table to 12 or 13 degrees and saw about 1/16 inch outside the line and you will leave behind enough wood to work with.

Most bandsaws, even mine with a 6-inch depth of cut, will make an easy job of it. Saw around the plan-view lines you drew on the top surface of the pattern, the length of both sides of the plug. (See Figure 2-10.) Now the plug is starting to look like a dory. (See Figure 2-11.) But flip the plug upside down and you will see that there is plenty of wood left at the bottom of the plug, outside the chine, which is what we intended.

Trimming and Fairing the Sides

The excess wood can be removed with a drawknife for rough work, and a spokeshave and low-angle block plane for closer tolerances. Before getting started, however, we need to make body patterns so we can determine the shape of the sides of the plug at each frame station. Three patterns are required for the four frame stations — one for Stations 2 and 3, which are the same shape, and one each for Stations 1 and 4.

Cut these roughly as before from the body sections on Sheet One, stick them to Masonite or aircraft plywood, and fair the working edges. Leave a couple of inches extra on the non-working edges so you can hang on to the patterns in use.

This is a good time also to make the patterns for the frames, the stem, the breasthook, and the transom knee. As with the transom pattern, add a little extra to the top of the stem to provide wood for shaping and beveling.

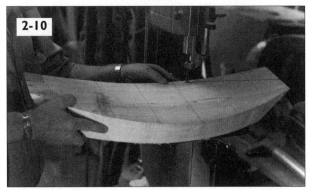

2-10 *Sawing the plan view on the bandsaw. Set the tilt of the table to 12 to 13 degrees, and saw with the top of the plug up. Concentrate on what you are doing. Make sure the direction of feed will produce a cut that angles in the right direction — in other words, when you have made your cuts, the sides of the plug will angle in toward the bottom centerline. Misjudge the direction of feed, and the sides will angle out — and you will have one strange-looking dory model.*

2-11 *The plug is starting to look like a dory. Note that the station lines have been re-established on the top. The key to making an accurate, symmetrical plug is to immediately redraw lines that are lost from sawing and shaping.*

2-12 *A sharp drawknife is used to hog off excess wood. Later, when working to really close tolerances, switch off to your spokeshave, block plane, and sanding blocks. Watch the grain so you don't dig in and pull off a huge splinter that might ruin the piece.*

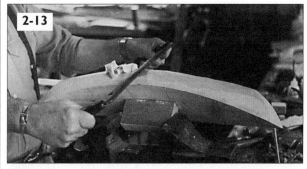

2-13 *Fasten a block of wood to the top of the plug so you can use it to hold the work securely in your bench vise. Reset the work as necessary, so you can work comfortably and see what you are doing.*

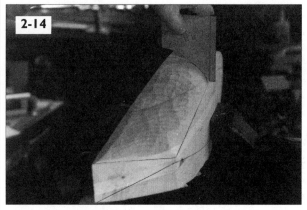

2-14 *Using a body pattern at the appropriate station to check the shape of the side. There's lots of daylight showing, but don't become overeager and go too far too quickly. Work the sides down gradually, checking as you go. Note that I have darkened the lines defining the transom and the bottom so I can keep track of them.*

With all your patterns made, you can now start shaping the sides. (See Figure 2-12.) To steady the plug while you do this, cut a scrap block of wood shaped to the profile of the sheer, glue it to the top surface of the plug, and use it to hold the plug in a vise. (See Figure 2-13.)

The idea when using the body patterns is to work wood off the plug until you are at the point of trying each pattern at the appropriate station. Don't try to make the pattern fit the station perfectly at one crack. (See Figure 2-14.) Work the sides down until the patterns almost fit at the frame stations, then blend and fair the sides along their length, then go back and work down the sides at the stations more closely to the patterns, then blend and fair the sides, etc. Eventually, you will reach the point where the patterns fit the stations perfectly, and the sides are faired from bow to stern.

That's the theory. Here's the practice:

With a spokeshave and block plane, fair the top edges — the sheer — of the plug along the lines that established the plan view.

With a drawknife first, followed by a spokeshave and a block plane, get rid of the ample amount of wood left around the chines.

With the sheer and the chine lines established, we have two precise lines to work to, and the rounding of the sides can begin.

Keep your body section patterns handy as you go and try them in place well before you will actually need to use them. Form a mental picture of the hull's shape at each frame station. This will program your mind and your hands to how much wood you can safely take off before you get to the final lines. Hold the patterns square to the centerline at each frame location. Reestablish the station lines as they disappear in the carving process.

When all four stations are very close to their final shape — in other words, the body section patterns almost fit — and the ends are very close as well, switch from your carving tools to sandpaper. Make a pad with 60-grit sandpaper and sand from the sheer to the chine across the grain, which will remove humps and hollows in this direction. Then, with a flexible batten with 60-grit sandpaper glued to it, sand the hull in a fore-and-aft direction. (See Figure 2-15.) Be careful when working at the ends that you do not round them off; they should finish with crisp, sharp lines.

When you are satisfied that all the bumps and hollows have been faired out in both the sheer-to-chine direction and fore and aft, switch to 100-grit paper, then to 180-grit, which is plenty fine enough for a plug.

Before calling the job done, sweep the hull with a small, clean batten, eyeballing any humps or hollows you may have missed. (See Figure 2-16.) For some reason or other, perhaps because I'm so cautious at the ends when carving and sanding to avoid whacking off too much, it's

2-15 *Fairing the sides with a homemade sanding board made of a thin backing strip with blocks glued to the ends to provide handholds. When making yours, follow this adage: the longer the board, the fairer the results.*

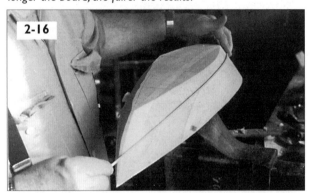

2-16 *Search for humps and hollows by sweeping the plug with a batten. Then run your fingers over the surface; you will be surprised by how much more you can "see" by touch than by eye.*

at the ends where my batten finds humps. (The other suspect areas are between the stations.) I've learned from experience: I spend extra time at the ends of the plug, so when I plank the dory, the planks flow along the hull smoothly out to the ends.

When you are satisfied that the plug is as accurate as you can make it, give it a sealer coat of shellac thinned 50 percent with solvent alcohol. (See Figure 2-17.) This sealer will dry in only a few minutes and is worth the effort, as it can save you from soiling the plug or worse.

What's worse? I didn't follow my own advice when making a demonstration plug. I drew the station lines first with a pencil, then traced over them with a ballpoint pen to darken the lines for the camera. Something in the ink of the pen bled out into the grain of the wood when I coated the plug with shellac. The lines went fuzzy. If I had followed my own advice and shellacked the plug as soon as I had finished shaping it, I would have avoided the mess. Ever watchful Mr. Murphy is alive and well.

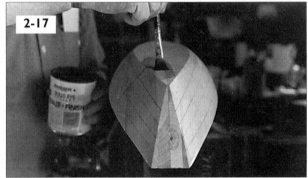

2-17 *Seal in any sap from bleeding knots and seal out future dirt by applying a coat of shellac thinned with alcohol. I use a lot of shellac when making models, because it does its job well and dries quickly.*

LINING OFF THE PLANKS

When contemplating the planking process, think of an orange — the sections all evenly divided, tapered, and beveled. If a fruit tree can do it, so can you.

This dory model will be planked with five strakes on each side, just like the original. The position of these planks must be marked on the plug before you start planking. And before you start determining the position of those planks, you must have station lines on the plug, so re-establish them if you haven't already. (See Figure 2-18.)

Of course, the shapes of the planks have been predetermined for you by the plank patterns drawn on the plans, but the location of the planking lines must be drawn on the plug to guide you in the planking process. This doesn't mean you can't vary the lie of these plank

2-18 *Use your body patterns to re-establish the station lines on the plug. Make sure the pattern is square to the centerline before tracing off.*

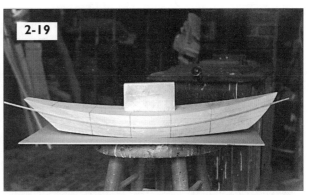

2-19 *A long flexible batten is used to mark off the lines of the planks. Drive tiny pins at the marks, and hold the edge of the batten against them. Before drawing a line, eyeball the batten for fairness and adjust it as necessary.*

lines a little. Each builder's plug is likely to vary somewhat from the prototype, but if you are reasonably close when lining off the planks, the final result will be accurate within reason.

Note that the planking lines are shown in a number of places on the plans. You can see them on the body section and hull profile drawings on Sheet One, and on the patterns for the transom, the stem, and frames 2 and 3 on Sheet Two. These are excellent guides for laying out your planking. For example, to mark the plank lines at Station 3, all you have to do is hold the Number 3 body pattern against the plug with the sheer mark matching that of the plug, and mark off each plank height at that station.

Note that the planking heights of the hull profile are so close for both Stations 2 and 3 that you can use the same frame pattern again and in the same way for Station 2. Mark the plank heights on the stem and the transom ends, and you have it made. Forget plank heights for Stations 1 and 4; the height locations just given are enough for the lining-off job.

Cut yourself a ¹⁄₁₆-inch by ¼-inch by 29-inch batten and spring it around the plug to locate the top of the garboard. You will need pins for this, the smallest you can find. The batten should pass through the marks for the top of the garboard in a fair curve; if it does not, adjust the batten until it does. Repeat this for planks 2, 3, and 4, and for the sheerstrake, on both sides of the hull. (See Figure 2-19.)

When you are done, take a hard look at the planking lines. See that the sides have been divided up equally into planks with equally spaced, faired lines. If you don't like what you see — if the planks don't seem equally spaced to your eye — then shift the marks slightly and spring your batten again. The plank height marks are there as a guide, not as an absolute; your eye should be the final judge.

MILLING OUT MODELING STOCK

Now that the planking lines are on the plug, we are closing in on the planking process. This is a good time to talk about milling out wood to model scale.

Saw Blades

The planking stock, whatever the species, is sawn out on a table saw with a hollow-ground combination planer blade. Hollow ground means the outer rim of the blade is thicker than the center. Such a blade has no set to the teeth, which is why it can cut smoothly — so smoothly that if the saw is tiptop sharp, no sanding is needed in the best of circumstances; in the worst, a few swipes with 220-grit will clean up the surface beautifully.

Hollow-ground blades tend to dull fairly quickly. Sawing out enough stock for a dozen of these Friendship clam dory models would likely slow down the blade's top cutting ability. I sharpen my own saws. (I also wrote a book about the process: *Keeping the Cutting Edge*, WoodenBoat Books, Brooklin, Maine.)

I get out my sharpening files when the blade tells me it needs to be sharpened. How does the blade do that? It won't make a parallel cut when I am pushing a stick through the table saw. The cut starts off fine, but gradually the stick binds against the fence, causing someone new at this sawing business to think the fence is out of whack. That's not likely to be the cause if the wood had been going through the saw okay before. Examination of the teeth of the blade by eye and fingers says they are sharp, but don't you believe it. The teeth are dull. Put a new, sharp blade on the machine, and you will see that sawing problem disappear.

I enjoy sawing out my own planking, and I'm pleased that I can make my table saw do what I want it to. You can be sure that if I can get a carbide-toothed saw to do as fine work as my hollow ground planer blade I'll buy one. So far I haven't found such a blade. I own three carbide-toothed blades that cut very well, but they rattle just enough in the saw kerf to leave the wood a bit rough, needing more hand sanding than I care to do. A nice thin-kerf carbide-tooth blade would be great because you would save on wood, but it is these very blades that do all the rattling. I like to think that some- day I'll run across a carbide-toothed saw that will do the job, but at 20 to 40 or so dollars a crack it is a bit expensive to keep sampling. And I see no offers in tool magazines to try one for free; neither have I seen any claims by saw manufacturers that their saws can match the smooth-cutting hollow-ground planer blade.

Saw manufacturers: Show me a saw that matches the smooth-cutting qualities of the hollow-ground combination planer blade. Make me eat my words!

Table Saws

What type of table saw is suitable for milling planking stock? I use an 8-inch Delta machine I bought nearly 50 years ago. It still serves me well. This saw was manufactured when pride of workmanship sold the product — not just a competitive price. It has a solid cast-iron ground-milled table, not these pressed-metal tables you see on most machines sold today. The mitre gauge is nicely made, very accurate, and doesn't rattle in the slot.

My old 8-inch Delta is a great saw. It does everything I want it to do, from sawing out parts for full-size boats to fine milling for the smallest boat models. If I were looking for a table saw today, I'd search the secondhand market for a carbon copy or something like it rather than settle for the sad quality of the average new 8-inch table saw.

Contrary to the advice you read in the modelers' magazines, an 8-inch table saw, not a miniature machine, is all you need to saw out modeling wood. A pint-size saw is fine for resawing wood that is already thin to begin with, such as stock that is $\frac{1}{16}$ inch or so thick. It'll do the job. But if you want a machine for cutting wood that is an inch thick or more to begin with, and saw plank after plank with it, a miniature table saw is useless.

A good 8-inch saw in practiced hands is capable of any model sawing job you want to do. My machine, fitted with an 8¼-inch blade, will cut a stick that is 2¼ inches thick and can saw a plank off that stick that is $\frac{1}{32}$ inch thick.

Sawing the Wood

Once you have the proper saw, sawing the wood to whatever size you need is easy. But study the stick first — pick it up, run it through your hands, eyeball it. Sight along the edges. If one edge is bowed a bit, put that edge against the fence and saw as many planks off the stick as you want. Your saw can handle a slight bowed curve like this, producing parallel planks, no problem.

If the piece of wood has a hollow curve on one edge, and if you put that edge against the fence, you will end up with a stick with thick ends and a thin middle. And the grain of the stick is likely to keep pulling to maintain the hollow even after many slices have been taken off.

Also study the wood for grain. You should run the stick through the machine so the saw cuts across the wood's growth rings, not parallel with them. Not only will the resulting stock look better, but also it will be more stable.

PREPARING TO PLANK

Let's go back to the model. Planking is coming right up, but first things first. We need a stem, a transom, and a bottom to hang the planking on.

The Stem

The shape of the stem is shown on Sheet Two. With your scale rule, you will see that it is sided 1$\frac{5}{16}$ inches. (Remember, that's the dimension of the stem on the full-sized dory; the dimension on the model is a fraction of that.)

What do I mean by "sided"? This is a boatbuilder's term that refers to the thickness of something in a side-to-side direction. Molded shape, on the other hand, refers to thickness in a front-to-back direction.

To hold the stem in place on the plug for planking, we must cut a pocket for it. This is very easy to do, but it must be done as accurately as possible. The stem, and the pocket for it, must be on the centerline and plumb to it. Our glued centerline serves us well for the job.

Begin by making a stem to the profile and sided dimension indicated on Sheet Two. Mill out a piece of stock that is big enough to make the stem in one piece and is 1$\frac{5}{16}$ inch thick as measured on the full-size boat. Using the profile of the stem on Sheet Two as a pattern, lay out the stem and cut it to shape.

Next, adjust the profile of the stem end of the plug so it matches the shape of the leading edge of the stem. The stem end of the plug should be cut away so it is square across; in other words, it should be flat, with a width on the flat that corresponds to the width of the stem. (See Figure 2-20.) That width should be split exactly down the middle by the glue line indicating the plug's centerline.

Now, make the pocket for the stem in the plug. The idea is to embed the stem in the plug, aligned and centered.

Cut the sides of the stem pocket with a fine-tooth saw — a razor saw is good — and a $\frac{3}{16}$-inch-wide

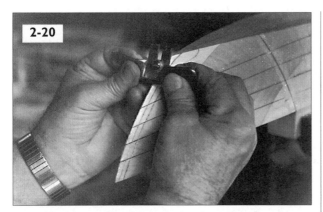

2-20 *After the profile of the stem has been drawn on the plug, the area is cut back to the line to create a flat. Here, I'm using a tiny spokeshave designed for making musical instruments; it's just as effective for fine-tuning dory models. Many of the specialty tool catalog outfits carry tools like this.*

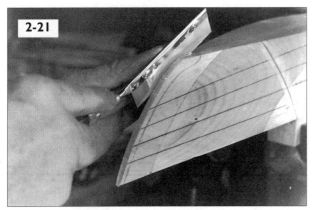

2-21 *A pocket to hold the stem embedded in the plug is cut by first running a razor saw down the side edges of the flat created in the previous step.*

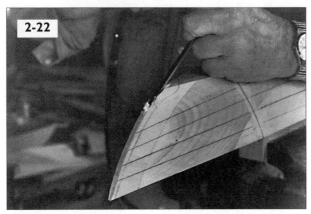

2-22 *A ³/₁₆-inch chisel is just right for removing the waste wood between the razor cuts for the stem pocket.*

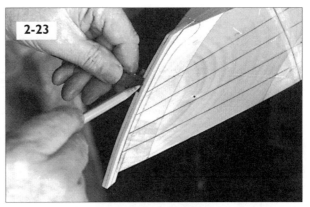

2-23 *The stem has been fitted in the pocket, with the foot of the stem flush with the bottom. A centerline is marked down the face of the stem to aid in beveling.*

chisel. (See Figure 2-21.) Be very careful to keep the saw blade aligned fore and aft with the centerline of the plug. There is no need to be fussy about the depth of the cut; all you are doing at this point is providing shoulders for the proper alignment of the stem in the plug.

Place the foot of the stem on the plug, holding it upright and centered, and mark around it. With a ³/₁₆-inch chisel, cut a pocket for it and the rest of the stem. (See Figure 2-22.) Cut a little and try a little until the stem sits in the pocket with a tight fit. The tight fit will hold the stem in place for beveling.

The foot of the stem should be flush with the bottom of the plug. The forward edge of the stem should protrude a little beyond the stem end of the plug. There's nothing critical about this; have enough showing to allow the gluing of the plank ends to the stem.

Draw a centerline down the face of the stem as a guide for your eye. (See Figure 2-23.) Both sides of the stem are now beveled so they fair into the sides of the plug. This is about as easy as anything can be. With a modeler's block plane you can do it right on the plug if the stem is reasonably tight in the pocket. After you take off what you can without cutting into the plug, switch to a sanding board and finish the bevel by following the curve of the sides of the plug. (See Figure 2-24.) Leave the stem a dite higher than the plug.

At this point, remove the stem and give the plug, with the exception of the top, a coating of heavy-duty silicone spray. This will prevent the side and bottom planking, and the transom, from being glued to the plug. Then put the stem back in its pocket in the plug.

The Transom

The transom knee will be fitted after the dory has

2-24 *The stem is beveled so it fairs into the sides, first with a small plane, then with a long sanding board. Note that I have faired back to the centerline of the stem on this side, and no farther.*

been planked and removed from the plug. The transom itself is made now.

The transom on the full-size dory is 1 inch thick and cut to the shape shown on the plans. Leave the top square across, 3 or 4 inches longer than necessary, and whack off the bottom tail to 1 inch wide. (The dimensions here are for the full-size boat; use your scale rule for the model.)

You can draw a centerline on the transom for alignment reference if you want, but it is hardly necessary once you get the transom on the plug. Your fingers will tell you when the overhang on either side of the plug is equal. After all, the average person can differentiate by touch two thickness of newspaper from one, which isn't bad. Don't be afraid to use your fingers for fine adjustments, and to trust them.

Using the same procedure as for the stem, bevel the side edges of the transom so they will follow the sides of the plug before mounting the transom on the plug. Guesstimate how much bevel to cut and finish the job on the plug.

Perhaps you would prefer to know the exact bevel, in degrees, of the transom edges. My bevel square says 42 degrees, which is interesting because it almost matches the transom bevel on Phil Bolger's Gloucester Light Dory — the Gloucester Gull — which is 42½ degrees.

How can I remember such an arcane number, since I haven't built a full-size Gloucester Gull for years? Probably having built 117 of them has something to do with it.

Hold the transom in place on the plug with pins. Three ought to do the job. Then extend the planking lines square across the transom as an aid in getting the plank ends at the same height on both sides of the boat.

By the way, if you want to finish your model bright,

any pin holes made in the transom or planking, or anywhere else, can be healed by dabbing with the end of a small stick soaked in water. To be effective, this must be done inside and outside the hull before it is sealed.

The Bottom

The bottom of the full-size dory is 1 inch thick and constructed of several planks cleated together. For the model, it is made of one piece of wood, with simulated planking seams scribed on it, and is installed before the garboard is fitted. If there is a transverse bow in the wood selected for the bottom put the bowed side on the outside of the hull.

Fitting the bottom is easy. Just saw it oversize, pin or tape it to the plug, and mark its shape from underneath, using the sides of the plug as a guide. (See Figure 2-25.) Saw out the bottom with your bandsaw set at 30 degrees; this safely leaves wood in the bow area, which has less bevel than the area near the stern, which has a bevel of 40 degrees. Sawing this much bevel now cuts down on hand planing later, so I'm all for it.

Before installing the bottom, permanently mark the frame locations on it and, with a needle and a straight-edge, scribe two caulking seams to simulate three planks. Note that on the full-size dory the center plank, at 12 inches, is the widest. Mark an X at the stern, so you can tell at a glance which end is which, because she widens at the stern. Mark the location of Frame 3 on the edge of the bottom; this mark is used to align the bottom on the plug.

If you haven't sprayed the plug with silicone to prevent the hull from bonding to the plug, do it now. Then put a dab of glue on the foot of the stem and on the bottom edge of the transom, and lay the bottom in place

2-25 *The stock for the bottom is laid over the bottom of the plug and kept from shifting temporarily with masking tape. The shape of the bottom is then marked on the stock, using the plug as a guide. What could be simpler?*

2-26

2-26 *A small plane is used to finish the bevel along the edges of the bottom so they fair into the sides, the stem, and the transom. Little modeler's planes are sold in most well-stocked hobby shops and by most specialty tool catalogs. Like all modeling tools, they must be kept sharp to be effective.*

on the plug. Wrap a piece of masking tape over each end to hold the bottom until the glue sets up. If the tape won't hold and you have to use pins, toe-nail them. Once the glue is dry, fair the edges of the bottom into the sides of the plug, and to the stem and the transom. (See Figure 2-26.)

That's it. Planking is next.

PLANKING

You can determine the shape of the planks yourself — i.e., spile them — or you can use the patterns on Sheet Two. If you use the patterns, cut them out all in one bunch, give the back of the paper a shot of spray glue, stick the patterns on Masonite, and cut them out individually.

The planking on the full-size Friendship clam dory is ⁹⁄₁₆ inch thick. Mill out a pile of planking stock to that dimension, scaled down to model size, of course; use your scale rule to be sure the thickness is accurate.

You will find a special, miniature planking bench a big help when cutting and beveling planks. Make your own by cutting a stick 29 or 30 inches long by 1½ inches wide by ½ inch thick, real measure, gluing this to a chunk of 2 by 4, and clamping the 2 by 4 in your vise.

The Garboard

The first plank we'll fit is the garboard, the lowermost side plank, so cut a piece of planking stock 2 inches wide by 25 inches long, real measure. We want something that won't bend edgewise. Align the piece just below the planking line of the top of the garboard — so the line shows — and tape it to each end of the plug. Don't pin or fasten the middle of the piece to the plug, as you want to be able to move the middle of the piece edgewise until it bears flat against the plug. The entire piece

must bear against the plug: at the ends, in the middle, everywhere.

Now we will determine the top edge of the garboard plank, which is what this piece of planking stock will become. For a marking batten, use the light batten you used to lay off the planking lines.

Lay the batten on the plug, aligned with the planking line of the top edge of the garboard. Measure the greatest gap between the batten and the edge of the template. Cut a small block a dite wider than the gap and slide it along the batten while marking the top edge of the planking stock. Or use a compass or dividers if you like. (See Figure 2-27.) Mark the location of Frame 3 on the planking stock before taking it off, so you can put it back exactly in place.

Remove the piece of planking stock, cut to the line you just scribed, and put the piece back on the plug to check for accuracy. If it looks good — if the top edge matches the planking line on the plug for the top edge of the garboard, and if the garboard is bearing everywhere — you're in business. Mark the bottom edge of the piece by tracing along the bottom of the boat and around the ends. Cut almost to the line; in other words, leave a little extra for trimming, then trim it.

You now have one garboard plank for one side of the boat. Trace around it onto another piece of planking stock for an identical plank for the other side of the boat.

Hang the Garboard

In boatbuilder's parlance, fastening a plank in place is called hanging it. That's what we will do here, but first the top edge of the garboard must be beveled for the lap; that is, the top edge of the plank must be prepared to receive the lower edge of the next plank, which will

2-27

2-27 *To spile the top edge of the garboard plank, I have used a compass to transfer the line of the batten to the planking stock. The batten and the planking stock can be temporarily held in place with masking tape or, as here, dressmaker's pins.*

overlap it just as a house shingle overlaps the one below it.

The full-size boat has a 1⅛-inch lap. In other words, the top edge of the garboard is overlapped by the lower edge of the next plank by that dimension, and for a waterproof seam at this overlap, the top edge of the garboard is beveled. The line of the lap must be marked, so make a marking gauge from a small piece of wood; the width of the gauge should be the scale width of the lap.

The bevel on the top edge of the garboard is made down to about one-half the thickness of the plank, but it can vary a little from this without any problem. The bevel remains the same along its length except at the ends. About 3 inches from the ends, the bevel is gradually increased until it produces a feather edge at the extreme ends of the plank at the top. This area of increased bevel is called the gain.

Be careful that you don't make the bevel wider while planing the gains. If you do, however, the chances are good that you won't have spoiled the whole show. When the hull is all planked up, a slightly wider bevel on a plank or two is unlikely to be noticed.

Beveling the top edge of the garboard plank is pretty much an eyeball operation. (The bottom edge does not have to be beveled.) I use a modeler's plane for this, and as I go I start rolling my wrist at the beginning of the gain and increase the roll as I near the end. The goal is to increase the angle of the bevel for a feather edge without increasing the width of the lap. (See Figure 2-28.)

It is unlikely you will plane by hand a perfectly flat bevel. More likely is that the surface will have a slight crown. If both plank bevels in a dory-lapped seam are crowned slightly, the planks won't lie properly and the seam will leak. Friendship boatbuilders took care of the problem in full-sized dories by using a round-soled spokeshave, which produced a slightly concave surface. To flatten a crowned bevel on your model, glue a piece of sandpaper to a short piece of ⅜-inch dowel and give the bevel a run along its length, paying special attention to the ends.

Keep in mind which side of the plug you are hanging the plank on and which side of the plank will be facing in and which out. Make reference marks to help you remember, as it is very easy to get the side you intended inside when you planned to put it outside, or the ends reversed. (Believe me, I have reason to know.) Garboards have so much shape that they are easier to keep track of, but Plank 2, the next plank up after the garboard, and all the rest have ends that are somewhat similar, but not quite. These planks must be marked so you don't hang them wrong end to or on the wrong side of the plug. Look and look again.

2-28 *Cutting the lap bevel on the top edge of the garboard plank. I use a modeler's plane for this, rolling my wrist to increase the bevel in the area of the gain. Note that I am supporting the long, thin plank on a homemade planking bench in a vise, and have immobilized the plank with clamps at each end.*

By the way, if you forget to bevel the top edge of a plank before you hang it on the plug, don't panic. (Yes, I know all about that, too.) Simply bevel the edge right on the plug. It might be more difficult than the recommended off-the-plug method, but it can be done.

Now give the garboard a dry run by holding it flat to the plug amidships and checking to see that the ends are aligned with the top edge of the garboard's planking line marked on the plug. Put a reference mark where the top edge of the garboard crosses Station 3, so you will be able to relocate the plank at its exact position when you are gluing it down. Without that mark, you will most likely be making a panic guess about where the plank should go. The odds are even that the plank will be stuck down in the wrong position, and then you will have a real mess on your hands.

Before spreading glue, remove the garboard and prepare several lengths of 1-inch masking tape for holding the plank on the plug. Masking tape is the best tool I know of for holding a plank in place while the glue dries. Cut your pieces long enough to run from one side of the plug to the other, across the bottom. Prepare as many as you need to do the job: masking tape is cheap.

I use Franklin Titebond for hanging the planks. It grabs quickly, which is a good feature. In warm weather it can be a little too quick, so to slow down the grab I'll thin the glue with a bit of water, which allows time to slide the plank around a fraction if last-minute adjustment is necessary.

Apply a light line of glue along the edge of the bottom planking and along the stem and transom, and hang the garboard. The tendency is for the top of the plank at the ends to spring away from the plug and for the middle of the palnk to slip edgewise toward the sheer. Stick the corner of a razor blade into the plug to prevent this and use the pull-power of properly positioned tape to hold it back. Begin taping amidships first, then work toward the ends, pushing the plank flat against the plug everywhere as you go.

While waiting for glue to dry, get the other garboard ready for the other side of the boat and trim the ends of the first garboard flush to the stem and the transom so they will not interfere with the ends of the second garboard. A single-edge razor blade is best for this. You should follow this procedure when hanging all the planks on both sides of the boat.

Hang the Remaining Planks

The next plank to hang is Plank 2, the next one up. Mark the lap line on the top edge of the garboard; this is for the bottom edge of Plank 2 to follow. (See Figure 2-29.)

Wrap a square-edge piece of stock, 29 inches by 1¼ inches by ⁹⁄₁₆ inch, real measure, around the plug. Make sure it lies flat on the plug everywhere, then scribe its bottom edge to follow the curve of the top edge of the garboard. Remove the piece, cut to the scribed line, and put the piece back on the plug with the bottom edge overlapping the garboard. You may have to adjust the curve slightly with your plane to get the piece to lie fairly. When satisfied with the fit, mark each frame location on the piece, which will become Plank 2, and remove it.

Set your dividers for the distance from the lap mark on the garboard to the line on the plug representing the top edge of Plank 2 at each station and at the bow and the transom. Transfer the top-edge marks to Plank 2, then spring a batten around them and scribe the

line. This line represents the top edge of Plank 2. Like the top edge of the garboard, it, too, must be beveled, as the rest of the planks (with the exception of the sheer plank) must be.

You need not bevel the bottom edge of Plank 2 to match the bevel on the top edge of the garboard, only the gains. The same applies to the rest of the planks. All you need is wood-to-wood contact in the lap. (See Figure 2-30.)

The procedure for hanging the rest of the planks is the same right up to the sheerstrake, the last one, which is slightly different.

The sheerstrake must be wide enough to extend ⅛ inch, real measure, above the top edge of the plug, so it should be made from a piece of stock 29 inches by 1⅜ inches by ⁹⁄₁₆ inch, real measure. (See Figure 2-31.)

2-30 *All but the sheerstrake has been hung. Careful lining off and fitting of the planks, and cutting of the lap bevels, produce a planking job that looks as real as anything done in Gloucester or Lunenburg in the old days.*

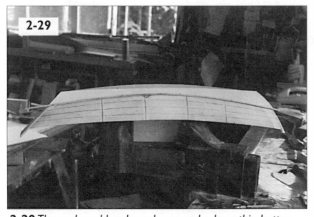

2-29 *The garboard has been hung, and a long, thin batten has been run along the plank to define the lap line to aid in the positioning of the next plank. Mark the line when you are satisfied it is fair.*

2-31 *The bottom edge of the sheerstrake is established just as the other planks, but excess wood is left on the top edge so it can be faired down to the top of the plug. As with all of the planks, it is glued in place by working from the middle toward the ends.*

Once it has been hung, on both sides of the boat, use the top edge of the plug as a guide to mark the curve of the top of the sheer.

REMOVE THE HULL FROM THE PLUG

Take a hard look at the sheerline: if it is less than perfect, cut a batten ½ real inch by 1/16 inch—long enough to extend from stem to transom. Spring this through the sheerline you just marked to fair it from humps or hollows.

Before taking your prize off the plug, mark the locations of the top of the frames. Just a slight dot with a pencil will do the job. (See Figure 2-32.)

Pull out any pins holding the hull to the plug; repair the holes by rubbing them with the end of a stick soaked in water. Cut the ends of the planking flush with the stem and the transom. Plane the bottom edges of the garboards flush with the bottom.

Remove the hull from the plug, and with the hull right-side up, mark each frame location from the sheer down to the inside bottom. Now you won't have to guess where the frames go. When we get around to fitting the frames, those on the starboard side of the boat are positioned forward of the line and those on the port side, aft of the line.

Now, at the frame stations, fit temporary cross spalls — spreader sticks — to push the sides back out to their proper lines. Without cross spalls, the sides collapse inward, thus decreasing the beam. Scale the length of each cross spall off the plans at the frame station where it will be fitted in the hull.

FINISH OFF THE HULL

Clean any glue lumps off the hull, inside and out, and sand away any uglies. Then prepare yourself mentally for many happy hours of cutting and fitting. An authentic scale-model Friendship clam dory will gradually emerge from a bare hull.

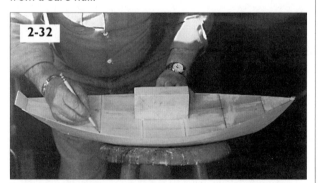

2-32 *The last thing to do before removing the hull from the plug is to mark lightly the locations of the tops of the frames on the edge of the sheerstrakes.*

Arch Board, Stern Knee, and Breasthook

The arch board is ⅞ inch on the full-size dory, and the end bevel is 40 degrees. Glue it in place. For accuracy, bore the holes for the rope becket on a drill press if you have one; if not, use a hand drill and be very, very careful.

The full-size stern knee is 1¹⁵/₁₆ inch thick. Fit your scale version and glue it in place.

The breasthook — the triangular piece with the curved back that fits in the bow behind the stem — is 1¾ inch in the full-size boat. It is notched for the stem. Because it has a slight crown, it is fitted so the top surface is ¼ inch, full-size measure, higher than the line of the sheer. The 1½-inch full-size measure left matches the thickness of the gunwale.

The angle of the sides of the breasthook where it fits the planking is 18 degrees; the angle at the stem is 40 degrees. To put in your model-size breasthook without tilting it one way or another, scribe a line around it to correspond to the ¼ inch measure on the full-size boat. Glue in the breasthook and cut the stem head flush to it.

Gunwales

The gunwales run along the inside of the top of the sheer. Their cross-sectional shape is shown on Sheet One of the plans. Note that the angled cut of the after corners of the breasthook are designed for a tight fit when installing the gunwales.

The cross spalls must be kept in place while the gunwales are fitted to maintain the hull's proper shape. Unfortunately, their ends, if not modified, will get in the way of the gunwales. To solve this problem, remove the cross spalls and notch their ends. (See Figure 2-33.) Drive pins in the ends of the cross spalls and cut them off almost flush. When you put the cross spalls back in place, the slightly protruding ends of the pins will keep them from sliding out of position. The dents made by the pins will be covered by the frames.

The gunwales are 1 inch by 1½ inches on the full-size boat. Sheet Two of the plans has a pattern for the gunwale and caprail together. You can use it and save yourself a lot of figuring, or go through the process with me and learn the fitting method for yourself.

You would think that laying a piece of cardboard across the sheer and tracing around the hull from underside would produce the shape of the gunwale, but it won't. The gunwale lies approximately square-edged to the flare of the sides amidships, but it must flatten out somewhat at the ends so the ends don't cock up too high. The gunwale must be, in a sense, spiled.

The easiest and most accurate way of capturing the

curve of the gunwale is with a plastic adjustable curve. Simply lay the device in the exact position you want the gunwale to lie, and you will have recorded the shape of the gunwale. (See Figure 2-33.)

The adjustable curve I used for this job is 32 inches long and 1 inch wide. It consists of 14 plastic laminations, bound together, that slide by one another easily enough to make quite a sharp curve, yet are stiff enough to hold the curve when you remove the device from the model. I bought mine in an artists' supply store about twenty years ago for $19.60. I'd gladly pay triple that for all the work it has saved. Besides my model work, I used it for taking the shapes of the frames off the old full-size dory.

Once you have the shape of the gunwale, grab a board 26½ inches long by 3½ inches wide by ¾ inch thick, real measure, and lay your gunwale pattern on it.

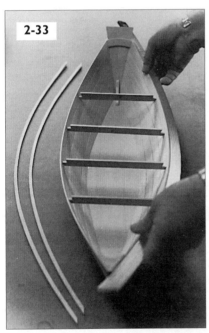

2-33 *A pattern from the plans can be used for the shape of the gun-wale, or you can take the shape right off the hull. For the latter, I am using a drafts-man's adjustable plastic curve. Note that the ends of the cross spalls have been notched so they can remain in place while the gunwale is fitted.*

Cut out the two gunwales on your bandsaw and smooth the outside cut as accurately as you can. Then resaw these strips for the scale thickness of the gunwales. You can do this freehanded, but I prefer to set up a wood fence on the table of my bandsaw and cut against that, as it eliminates any chance of "wee-waw." While you're at it saw a couple of extra pieces to use for the caprail; these should correspond to the 2½-inch width and ½-inch thickness on the full-size boat. (See the cross-sectional drawing on Sheet One.)

Note that the dory's side flare increases from amidships to the transom. Because of this, the after portion of the outboard edge of the gunwale must be beveled about 16 degrees so its end will match the

2-34 *The forward end of the gunwale fits against the after corner of the breasthook. Clamp the gunwale temporarily in place to mark the line.*

curve of the arch board. A lesser bevel — about 12 degrees — is required from amidships to the bow.

Caprails

The caprails on the full-size dory are ½ inch thick by 2½ inches wide, are sawed out square edged, and are glued down with instant glue. Note that the width at the forward and after ends of the full-size boat is 1¼ inch.

While the caprail in the full-size dory is made up of pieces, it is easier to make it in one piece for the model and simulate the joints by scoring with a razor blade. (See Figure 2-35.) Note that the after end is notched to butt against the arch board; the side is flush to the outside of the planking and ends flush to the outside of the transom (a razor blade will make this cut nicely). The fit at the after end is made first, and that at the forward end last. The forward end is mitered with the centerline and cut flush to the hull's stem profile. The joint is then covered by the false stem.

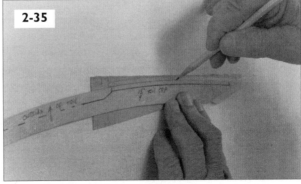

2-35 *Use the caprail pattern to mark your stock. As everywhere in the dory, to look right, the lines must be fair, so make sure your pattern is fair before you use it.*

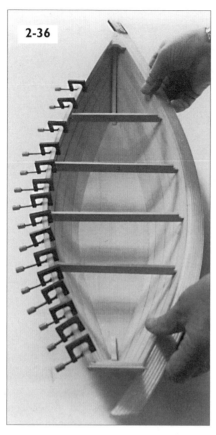

2-36

2-36 A long line of modeler's clamps is holding one gunwale in place, while an adjustable curve is being used to show how the shape of the gunwale was determined.

To clamp the gunwales and caprails while the glue sets, and for other modeling purposes, I use clamps made by R. Ullom Co. (See Figure 2-36.) In my view these are the Cadillac of clamps and are a pleasure to use. Their movable foot pads even allow clamping slightly beveled surfaces, which comes in handy. Unfortunately, Ullom no longer makes the clamps which is a loss to modelers. Isn't that the way all things go?

At the other end of the price scale, you can buy miniature wooden clothespins from Walmart or other discount outlets for about 2 bucks a dozen. These make excellent clamps.

It is very difficult to glue a long, thin stick of wood with Titebond or any other quick-grabbing glue. The glue usually grabs before the piece has been properly positioned along its length, and the piece cannot be moved without making a mess. In situations like this, particularly for gluing the gunwales and rubrails, I clamp the piece exactly where I want it and then apply very thin glue to the seam; the glue seeps into the seam and sets up. Titebond isn't very thin glue, so for an operation like this I switch to instant glue (cyanoacryolate). I use two types: very thin, like water, which will wick into the tightest of joints, and thicker, which is good for less tight-fitting joints.

Frames

We're finishing her up fast. The frames are next.

On the full-size boat, the frames are made of two pieces, gusseted at the joint with diamond irons. For our model, using the patterns, we can make them in one piece and simulate a joint at the knuckle by scribing with a razor blade and fitting a miniature diamond iron.

Make the frames $\frac{1}{8}$ inch thick, real measure. For stock, use a piece of $1\frac{3}{4}$-inch by 23-inch basswood. For sanding the inner curves, use fingernail emery boards.

The diamond irons can be made from thin .005 mm brass sheet, available from most hobby shops. You could also go to your local newspaper and ask them for scrap aluminum printing plates. These plates are thin, easily cut, and usually free. They have all sorts of uses in model-making and elsewhere as well: Some of our local ice fishermen use them for sheathing their ice shacks.

Thin brass, aluminum printing plates — either can be cut with ordinary household scissors. To make up a bunch of diamond irons, I cut one to shape, glue it on the end of a stick, and use it as a pattern to mark the rest. The irons are riveted to the frames in the full-size dory; you can simulate this effect by pressing a needle point against the backside of the iron, following the fastening pattern shown on the plans. Then glue the irons to the frames. (See Figure 2-37.)

When you fit and install the frames, remember that those on the port side lie aft of the frame lines you drew some time back and those on the starboard side forward of the lines. The frames will require beveling and sanding so they lie properly. Don't forget the limber holes; cutting them before the frames are glued in place is a lot easier than afterwards. When the frames have

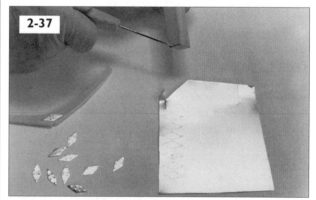

2-37

2-37 Diamond irons for the frames can be made from sheet brass or aluminum, traced on with a pattern glued to the end of a stick. Fastenings can be simulated by pressing the point of a needle into the back of the iron.

finally been inserted in the boat, work their tops in a little at a time under the gunwale until their bottoms lie flat against the bottom of the dory.

Instant glue is good for holding the frames in place. I use ZAP "super fast cure," a type of tacking glue that does exactly what it says it will. Leave the cross spalls in while putting in the frames; remove them after the glue has dried.

Thwart Risers

The pattern for the thwart risers, which support the thwarts, is on the bottom of Sheet Two. Note that they taper from the middle toward the ends. As they are $\frac{9}{16}$ inch thick, you can make them from leftover stock for the planking. There is no need to bevel the top edge; leave them square-edged.

The tops of the risers on the full-size dory are positioned against the inside of the frames at a point 9¾ inches down from the top of the gunwales at Frames 1 and 4. The shape of the risers will then take their proper lie against the inside of Frames 2 and 3.

Risers are cranky things to install. They should be fastened in the middle first, then the ends. When you are done, all that will be left is fairing the breasthook to the gunwales, cutting the top of the transom to shape, putting in the bottom cleats, fitting the caprails and thwarts — well, that sounds like a lot of work, but it's not that difficult or time consuming.

Bottom Cleats

The bottom cleats extend across the inside bottom of the boat, in the spaces between the frames on 1-foot 4-inch centers in the full-size boat. The ends are kept back from the garboards by ¾ inch, full measure, for waterways. These cleats are simple pieces, but it is surprising how much they add to the finished look of the dory.

False Stem

The false stem covers the forward edge of the stem. A pattern for it can be found on Sheet Two. Saw it out square edged, draw a centerline on it, and glue it in place with Titebond, aligning the centerline of the false stem with the centerline of the stem. Hold it in place with masking tape or pins. After the glue has hardened, remove the tape or pins and fair the sides of the false stem into the sides of the hull. (See Figure 2-38.)

Gunwale Straps

The gunwale straps fasten the top of the frames to the gunwale. These are made from .005 mm brass sheet or aluminum printing plate, with simulated fastenings top and bottom. In the full-size boat the top ends of the straps were bent over the gunwale and covered by the caprail. For the model, the tops are fitted flush under the caprail and let slightly into the gunwale so nothing will catch on them. This is easier to do and has the added bonus of looking better. Use a razor blade to let the straps into the gunwale.

The Top of the Transom

To mark the crown at the top of the transom, establish a centerline on the outside of the transom, set your compass or dividers on this centerline, and swing the arc. (See Figure 2-39.) Follow the same procedure on the inside.

Be very careful when cutting down the transom; you don't want to take too much off. It is rounded to an arc from side to side and faired to the caprails. (See Figure 2-40.) The final shape does much to establish the handsome lines of this dory.

2-38 *The false stem is sawn out square edged and glued to the stem. Fair it into the side planking with a small plane.*

2-39 *A compass is used to mark the arc of the top of the transom.*

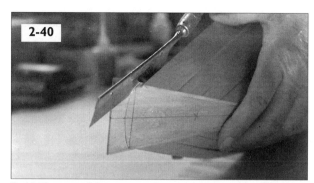

2-40 *The top of the transom has a strong reverse bevel, so be very careful when cutting the curve. The safest way to do this is to have the outside face of the transom facing you as you cut.*

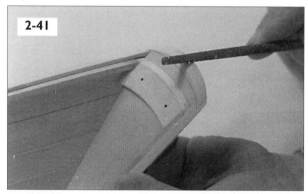

2-41 *Cutting a sculling notch is a fiddly job and may not seem worth the trouble, but that tiny semicircle helps make your dory model look "real." Use a rattail file. Here, you get a good view of how the gunwales and caprails finish off at the stern.*

The top of the transom is a reverse bevel, so keep your eye on the outside line as you work the crown. If you mark and cut from the outside to the inside, you will likely do okay.

File a sculling notch in the transom with a ⅛-inch rattail file, and the job is done. (See Figure 2-41.)

Thwarts

The Friendship clam dory has 4 thwarts, 1 inch thick by 8 inches wide on the full-size boat, the patterns for which are shown on Sheet Two. Note that they are notched at the ends to fit around the frames, and that the notches are staggered because the frames on the starboard side of the boat are slightly ahead of the frames on the port side. Draw a centerline on each thwart to keep track of this.

I use a modeler's square file to adjust the notches so the ends of the thwarts will fit over the frames.

Fit the thwarts, but don't glue them in yet, as they will be removed when the inside of the hull is painted.

Rubrails

The rubrails are ⅝ inch by 1¼ inches on the full-size dory and half round in section. Normally, I would be inclined to put them on square edged and round the corners, but to be authentic, you should make them up as half rounds to begin with.

The easiest way I know of to make half-round rubrails is to buy two ³⁄₁₆-inch birch dowels and saw to the centerline of each on a table saw. You need two, because half of each dowel is destroyed by the kerf of the saw blade. To keep the dowel from chattering and rotating while it is run through the table saw, use two wooden featherboards — one pushing down from the top and the other pushing in from the side.

Clamp the rubrails in place and glue them with thin instant glue run into the seams.

False Bottom

The best time to lay on the false bottom is before the hull is removed from the plug. The false bottom on the full-size boat was made of well-soaked beech, left unpainted, and was sacrificial to protect the inner bottom. The old-timers soaked the wood first, because they knew from experience that the false bottom would buckle in use if it were put on dry. Of course, your model dory will never see the water, so you false bottom needn't be soaked. (See Figures 2-42 and 2-43.)

2-42 *The false bottom is fitted the same way the bottom was: by laying the stock on the bottom of the hull and marking around the line of the chine. Glue the false bottom to the bottom.*

2-43 *Use long strips of masking tape to hold down the false bottom while the glue dries. Masking tape is a modeler's friend — useful as a clamp, temporary fastening, extra hand, surface protector, and more.*

2-44 *For a clear finish on the interior, apply a couple of coats or more of thinned shellac, then a top coat of polyurethane spray. Removable thwarts make the job easy.*

Final Details

The irons at the foot of the stem and the transom are made from .005 mm brass sheet or aluminum printing plate. Pin and glue them in place.

The holes on each side of the bow for the painter are 5/64 inch, real measure. Use the painter hole jig on Sheet Two as a guide for positioning them properly. The same size holes are drilled in the top of the transom for the lifting becket.

PAINTING AND FINISHING

All old-style dories, including the Friendship clam dory, are workboats and are therefore painted all over, inside and out, in one color. But for a mantelpiece model you would likely be forgiven if you finished her clear inside to show off your excellent building details. A fine-looking finish is white paint outside, with clear rubrails.

As I make dory models professionally, the buying public picked the painting scheme for me. I started out building Banks dory models, the type described in the next chapter. I had in mind a great fleet laid out on a table. I wanted to paint each boat in my fleet a different color, and I did. I even painted one bright orange inside and out. As a kid I remembered seeing dories of that color perched atop the wheelhouses of the fishing draggers in my home port of Rockland, Maine. They were used as lifeboats long before rubber rafts came along; the bright orange paint was for heightened visibility in an emergency.

I had green dories, gray dories, and white dories. I even had a bunch of mustard-yellow Banks dories, the traditional color of those built in Lunenburg, Nova Scotia.

I was especially proud of the mustard-yellow ones, as my full-size boatbuilding image was tainted a bit by the quick-and-dirty Instant Boats I built by the dozen. Here was my chance to show the world that I knew what "real" down-home traditional boats looked like.

Boy, was I in for a surprise. My models painted to look like workboats didn't sell. When I finished them to look like yachts, they did.

Anyone for a nest of mustard-colored Banks dories? Or perhaps you would prefer flaming orange?

My choice for a clear interior is a couple of coats of thinned shellac; more coats are even better. (See Figure 2-44.) Sand between coats. Finish off with a coat or two of fast-drying polyurethane, which is available in a spray can from Minwax. This provides protection from handling and evens out any glossy spots, leaving a satin glow that is somewhere between glossy and flat. (See Figure 2-45.)

For painting the outside, I use flat white acrylic, a fast-drying water-based craft paint available at Walmart and other outlets. Such paint comes in a huge variety of colors, which can be mixed to make even more colors. Acrylic paint is easy to use and produces an excellent finish. It's the way to go.

Even Micro Mark, suppliers of modeling tools and materials for years, including their highly touted Floquil paints, called their new line of Accu-flex water-based acrylic paints "revolutionary" when they were introduced. Here's some of what they had to say: "At first we thought 'revolutionary' was too strong a word for describing a new line of model paints. But after seeing it demonstrated at a trade show and testing it ourselves

2-45

2-45 The interior of the Friendship clam dory, all finished out and ready for accessories.

My procedure is to lay down a couple of coats with a conventional brush, followed by a couple more with an air brush. The preliminary brush coats are to drive the paint into the hairline seams of the boat. Air brushing won't do this. My air brush is a Paasche from Micro Mark and cost about $50, plus another $80 or so for a small compressor. This is not a top-of-the-line airbrush, but it is good enough to produce a finish that will impress anyone who sees it. The Paasche has so little overspray that you can hold a part in your hands and paint it without fear of spraying the whole room. Cleaning and care is easy. Shoot water through it for the first cleaning and lacquer thinner for the last.

EXTRAS THAT MAKE A DIFFERENCE

Since the model looks this good, let's go whole hog and add the finishing touches: oars, oarlocks, a wooden scoop for bailing, a rope becket in her transom, a painter, and a cradle.

Oars

The proper full-size length of oars for this boat is 8 feet. Make them of basswood to the shape indicated on Sheet Two of the plans. Note that there are two oar patterns, one for the plan view (looking down on the oar from above) and the other for the side view. Note also that the shaft of these oars is not uniform in thickness; rather, it tapers in both directions.

Get out a piece of model stock that corresponds to the 8 foot long by 7 inch wide by 1¾ inch thick lumber used for full-size oars. Lay your plan-view pattern on the stock, trace around the pattern, saw out the oar, and sand the edges. (This is a pair of oars, so make an identical mate to this first one as you go.) (See Figure 2-46.)

we were convinced that it truly is a revolutionary product! Because it's water-based it has no foul odor, dries fast, cleans up quickly and easily with water, is nontoxic, nonflammable, and nonirritating. It adheres extremely well to almost all materials including wood, plastic, pewter, steel, aluminum, brass, lead, fiberglass, casting resin, plaster, Delrin, rubber, glass, textiles, porcelain, and paper. Metals need to be cleaned of oil. Primers are not necessary!" They go on to say while touting their own brand, "Accu-flex is also very tough and flexible, gives complete coverage with a total thickness of just .001, so doesn't hide tiny rivets and other small details. Dries to touch in 3 to 5 minutes, is ready to mask and repaint in 20."

That's right up my alley — easier and faster to use, and doesn't sacrifice quality. So I, along with fellow modeler Peter Spectre, who told me about using acrylic paints in the first place, have joined the revolution and switched over from solvent- to water-based paints. But with a slight difference. We get ours right down the road in the hobby section at Walmart and pay about a buck for 2 fluid ounces of craft paint instead of about three bucks for 1 fluid ounce formulated for model making. Properly used, there isn't a dime's worth of difference between the two.

As for application, we thin it with water about 50-50 for spraying. The paint is okay straight from the bottle for brushing, even though it looks too thick for that. Peter, however, much prefers to thin his down considerably and lay on more coats for opacity.

2-46

2-46 Sawing out the oars on a bandsaw. Be sure you mark the centerline in both plan and profile views, as it is indispensable for making the oars straight and symmetrical.

Now for the side view. Mark a centerline along the side edge of the oar, lay on the side-view pattern, aligning it with the centerline, and trace the shape. Lay the oar flat on your workbench, with wooden stops at each end of the oar to prevent it from sliding away from you. With a plane, work down the blade on both sides to its proper thickness. Then, begin tapering the loom, or shaft. First 8-side the loom, then 16-side it, then make it round. Fair the loom into the blade as you go, and fine-tune the blade itself. Note that the blade tapers in two directions: to the tip, and to the edges. Before working on the hand grip, sand the oar with 180-grit paper, then 220, then 320.

To hold the loom in a vise without damaging it while working on the grip, bore a ¹⁵⁄₆₄-inch hole, real measure, through a block of wood, then split the block down the center. Sandwich the loom in the split block, and put the block in the vise. (See Figure 2-47.)

Now finish the grip. Don't just guess where the end

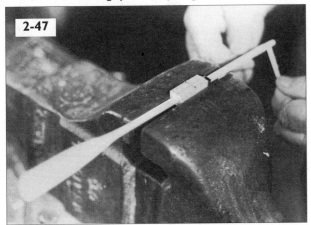

2-47 *A block of wood with a hole in it, split in half, holds the loom of the oar in a vise while you shape the grip.*

of the grip should be. Check the centerline, then draw a circle to represent the end. Work to this final shape.

That's the old-fashioned way of rounding the loom and the grip. Now, with a relatively inexpensive accessory for a ⅜-inch reversible variable speed drill, the job can be substantially easier. The accessory is a small 3-foot lathe from Leichtung. It is 26 inches between centers and will take workpieces up to 6 inches in diameter. (See Figure 2-48.)

You don't need cutting tools to turn the loom of a tiny dory oar. A mill file and sandpaper will do the job. A standard four-spur drive center is too big for the oar, so to hold it in the chuck, cut a piece of copper tubing and chuck it in the drill. Cut the stock for the oar longer both at the grip and the blade ends, jam the grip end

2-48 *This is a nice little rig for turning your workbench into a miniature oar shop. It's a 3-foot lathe driven by an electric drill.*

tightly in the copper tubing, tighten the live center on the blade end, and away you go.

This little lathe is a delight to use. The only part of the oar you will have to finish by hand is the blade.

When you have finished both oars, give them a final sanding, a couple of coats of shellac — sanding between — and a coat or two of polyurethane spray.

Some dory oars were left unprotected. Others were protected from chafe with leather or wrappings of twine where they worked in the thole pins or oarlocks; a thicker wrapping, the button, prevented the oars from sliding out of the oarlocks when unattended.

If you decide to add this ultimate detail, you have a choice of leather or twine. I always use twine — thicker nylon for the button, thinner for the protective covering — glued in place and coated with white paint. (See Figure 2-49.) If you prefer, the twine can be given a stain to simulate manila line; BlueJacket Ship Crafters sells a stain especially for this purpose.

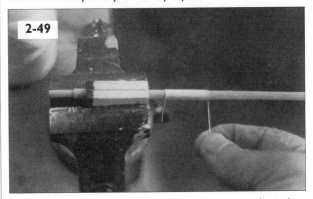

2-49 *Wrapping an oar with light line to protect it where the loom chafes in the oarlocks. To give this ultimate authentic touch a more authentic touch, darken the line with stain to simulate manila.*

Oarlocks

The shape of the oarlocks is shown on Sheet Two. I made my first pair from a brass door kick protector plate I picked up at a lawn sale. If you don't have any such scrap brass lying around, you can use new brass stock from your local hobby shop. You can saw it by hand with a hacksaw or on a bandsaw with a fine-toothed blade.

Oarlock-making can be difficult and time consuming. It can take a couple of days to make a pair, and it is not easy to make the two oarlocks identical.

First make a pattern of the oarlock from thin stock, such as modeler's brass plate. When you are satisfied with the shape, trace around it with a scratch awl, then cut to the mark. Leave a temporary leg on the oarlock to hang onto while you work it down. If, while you are cutting to the line, the brass is so bright you can't see the scratch mark, give the surface a swipe with a color marker, then re-scratch the line.

Be prepared to spend a day making one oarlock, though you can speed up the job by boring out the waste between the two horns of the oar with a $\frac{9}{32}$-inch bit. This will eliminate quite a lot of brass fast. From here on, a set of modeler's files works well. You will need three shapes at least: round, triangular, and oval.

Before filing the edge-taper of the horns, be sure to strike a centerline so you won't have the horns leaning one way or the other. And before rounding the end of the shank, remember to drill a hole for the keeper. (The keeper is a length of chain used to prevent the oarlock from going adrift when it is not seated in the oarlock socket.)

The easiest socket arrangement is to bore a hole through a piece of flat brass, set the plate on the caprail, and drill through the hole in the plate down into the caprail to accommodate the oarlock shank. (See Figure 2-50.) You could also make a side mounting, but this would call for more machining and filing, adding many, many more hours to the job.

I can't say as I would ever want to make more than one pair of these oarlocks. Since I build model dories by the boxful, I gave my prototype pair to BlueJacket Ship Crafters and they made a mold from them. You can therefore buy a set of these oarlocks, with sockets, from BlueJacket. They are cast in Britannia metal, which will not corrode in a model case the way lead fittings will. If you want to simulate galvanized oarlocks, leave the Britannia uncoated. If brass, dip the oarlocks in lacquer thinner or solvent alcohol to remove any mold residue that might prevent paint from sticking and paint them with gold spray paint.

Because the frames are staggered, locate the oarlock sockets 1 foot 7 inches from the after side of Frame 2 on the starboard side of the boat, and 1 foot 7 inches from the forward side on the port. This is full-size measure; scale it down for your model.

Painter and Becket

Both the bow painter and transom becket can be made from 3-strand nylon, approximately ⅟₁₆-inch, real measure. Reeve the line for the becket through the transom holes, apply a shot of instant glue to the ends of the line to keep them from unraveling, cut the tips cleanly with a razor blade, and tie stopper knots in the ends to keep them from pulling back out of the holes.

I leave my dory models painter-less, as it would require making an eye splice at the bow and that's a lot of extra work. I don't feel a painter enhances the final appearance of the model by the amount of effort required to make it. To my eye, the bow looks great as it

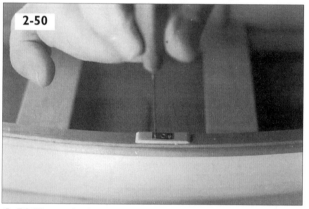

2-50 *The oarlock socket fits in a pad glued to the caprail. Fastenings can be simulated by drilling holes and driving in pins.*

2-51 *The last word in dory gear — a custom scoop for bailing her out. Use the patterns to make the parts and glue them together.*

is with just the holes for the painter. But don't let me hold you back. Go ahead and make that teensy eyesplice if you want.

Scoop

Before the invention of the cutoff plastic Clorox bottle, a wooden scoop, or bailer, used to be in every small boat afloat. Many were strictly functional, but others were pieces of folk art, each individually crafted for lightness, function, and good looks. The thinner the wood they were made from, the better they looked and worked. Some of the best were made from cedar shingles, but they tended to be less durable than those made from pine.

A pattern for a typical Friendship clam dory scoop can be found on Sheet Two. It has a flared mouth, a curved handle, and a partially closed-in top to form a pocket for water. (See Figure 2-51.) The sides, top, and bottom of the originals were the same thickness, about ¼ inch.

To make the scoop, first make the bottom, then the sides. The sides are glued to the bottom, so the bottom is between them, and the end piece is notched and glued to the sides and the bottom. The top goes on next, and then the handle is slipped into the notch, with the underside glued to the inside bottom of the scoop.

Cradle

Patterns for a cradle to hold your dory on display are indicated on Sheet Two. This cradle, which requires only three pieces, is quite handsome for something so simple to make. Make it from basswood, with a tight fit for the stretcher, and use instant glue to hold it together. This completes your beautiful Friendship clam dory.

Now that you have built this one, you have the experience to build the other two dories in this book.

Now here's one fine-looking dory, all fitted out and painted up, and ready to be launched into the 'Keag River for a day of clamming.

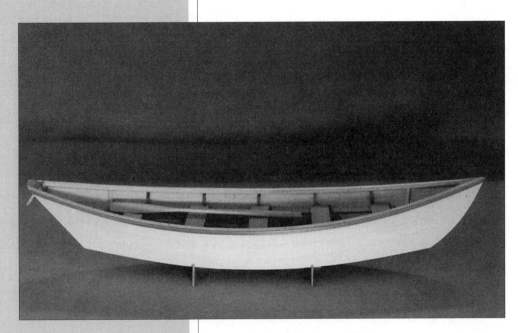

CHAPTER 3

The 14-foot Banks Dory

The Banks dory is a type, but there are many styles within that type. Of all the styles I've seen, I find the 14-foot Higgins and Gifford Banks dory, which used to be built in Gloucester, Massachusetts, to be the most eye-catching. The strong but graceful sheer, the cut of that hungry bow, the rake of the transom, those proportions so beautifully brought together — all of this taken together reeks of function and seaworthiness. That's why I built 30 or so models of the Higgins and Gifford dory before I could stop long enough to write about it.

The lines for this dory were provided by Howard I. Chapelle, who wrote in his book *American Small Sailing Craft* (W.W. Norton & Co., New York), the men of Higgins and Gifford "had great reputations for excellence in design and build. In fact, the model and construction of the Higgins and Gifford bank dory became the standard in the type by 1886 and was much copied."

So come along with me on this adventure, and we will copy in model form this most handsome of dories.

The model construction method for the Friendship clam dory and the Banks dory is basically the same — we will carve a plug and plank the model over it. The 14-foot Banks dory at 18 feet 1½ inches long (14 feet on the bottom, hence the name) is a bit longer than the Friendship, but if we build it at a scale of 1 inch equals 1 foot, the model will be a little shorter (18½ inches long versus 26½ inches for the Friendship), so that's what we will do.

Since the building technique for this dory is much the same as for the Friendship clam dory, I will skip over some of the material included in the last chapter. There's no need to repeat myself unless I'm trying to reinforce a point.

The 14-foot Higgins and Gifford Banks dory is easier to build than the Friendship clam dory. Whereas the Friendship clam dory has rounded sides, the Banks dory is straight sided, which means in shaping the plug you need only cut a straight line between the sheer and the chine for the entire length of the hull. The plug for the Banks dory is narrower than that of the Friendship, so you can get by with a bandsaw that has only a 6-inch depth of cut, rather than the 8 inches necessary for the Friendship.

To make the building process even easier, I planked the Banks dory with 3 strakes instead of the 4 shown on the plans for the original boat. This allows wider planks, which are easier to work with and hasten the planking process without detracting from the handsome

looks of the dory. I can easily plank up the hull of this model boat in about 3 hours, or two hulls in a short day, providing I have all the parts I need — planking, transom, stem, and transom knee — cut out beforehand. The tops of all 3 strakes are straight, providing nice planking lines, as easy as it gets — no hocus-pocus here.

The plans show 4 strakes rather than 3 only because they were drawn after the trees for wide planks had been virtually all used up, and Higgins and Gifford had to resort to narrower planks, and more of them, to fill out the sides. I don't feel as if I'm cheating with 3, then. At the scale we're working in, milling out wide planks is no problem. You can bet that the real dory builders, who had to turn out hundreds of boats a year, used 3 wide planks instead of 4 narrower ones whenever they had the stock to do it with.

There are as many ways to build this model as there are to build full-size dories, and you wouldn't be faulted for planking it and finishing it any way you wanted, borrowing the best from whatever source you chose. John Gardner in *The Dory Book* (Mystic Seaport Museum, Mystic, Connecticut) shows several different styles. For this model I made some minor construction changes, but I made absolutely no change in the hull lines. Higgins and Gifford, and Howard Chapelle, got them right for this one.

THE PLANS

Let's look at the plans, which consist of two sheets — Sheet One showing scale plans of the full-size boat, and Sheet Two containing patterns for making the model.

Again, the plans reproduced here are not to scale. To use them from the book, you can have them enlarged with a photocopier to whatever size you want. I will be describing how to build this model at 1-inch = 1-foot scale. Plans for building a dory at this scale can be purchased directly from me.

Sheet One indicates that the offsets are to the inside of the plank, which is nice to know. This means that you don't have to deduct the thickness of the plank when laying out the frames. You know that if you make the frames as shown in the body section, they will fit inside the dory.

Sheet One is for reference; we won't be working with that. Sheet Two is our real road map. By using all those patterns for the parts, and by using the hull profile directly as a pattern, Sheet Two allows us to build a model with hardly any measuring at all. That's simple

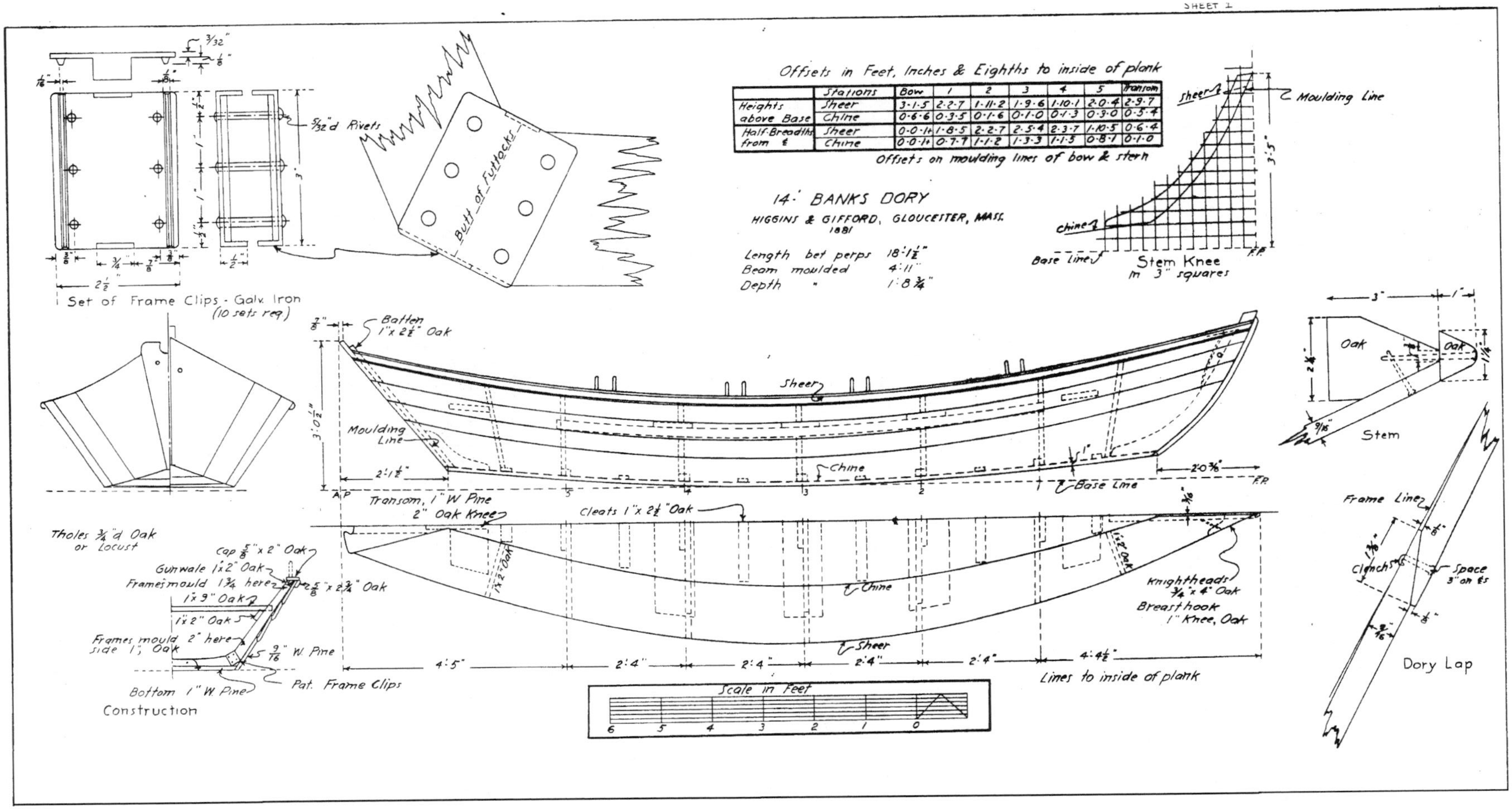

14' BANKS DORY

HIGGINS & GIFFORD, GLOUCESTER, MASS.
1881

Length bet perps 18'1½"
Beam moulded 4'11"
Depth " 1'8¾"

Offsets in Feet, Inches & Eighths to inside of plank

Stations		Bow	1	2	3	4	5	Transom
Heights above Base	Sheer	3:1:5	2:2:7	1:11:2	1:9:6	1:10:1	2:0:4	2:9:7
	Chine	0:6:6	0:3:5	0:1:6	0:1:0	0:0:3	0:3:0	0:3:4
Half-Breadth from ₵	Sheer	0:0:11	1:8:5	2:2:7	2:5:4	2:3:7	1:10:5	0:6:4
	Chine	0:0:11	0:7:7	1:1:2	1:3:3	1:1:3	0:8:7	0:1:0

Offsets on moulding lines of bow & stern

modelmaking — so simple, so easy, that it almost seems as if it can't be right. Believe me, I can tell you from experience that it is right.

Too often it's the easy way of doing things that eludes us. We have all done something the difficult way because we didn't know better. After much agony we found that the job could have been much simpler the first time around if we had thought more about it, or if we had more experience.

Stick with me on this one. The easy way and the right way will come the first time around.

Let's get at it.

MAKE THE PLUG

The plug on which this dory will be planked is carved from a rectangular block measuring 19 inches by 5½ inches by 3½ inches. This block can be laminated from whatever thicknesses of wood are required to make it. If you use ¾-inch pine, for example, you will need 8 pieces measuring 19 inches by 3½ inches. To make the plug, follow the instructions for the Friendship clam dory in Chapter 2. Remember, the center glue line in the block will be the centerline of your plug. (See Figure 3-1.)

With a pair of scissors, roughly cut out the hull profile from Sheet Two of the plans. Remember that to use the plans from the book, you must first enlarge them by photocopying. This is the side view of the dory, shown at the top of the sheet, just below the pattern for the oars.

Note the positioning of the frames on Sheet One. Frames 1 and 2 are positioned forward of the station lines, and Frames 3, 4, and 5 are aft of them. To remind

yourself of that later, when you fit the frames in the model, mark the location of the frames at the stations on the hull profile pattern with a red pen or a highlighter.

Give the hull-profile pattern a shot of spray glue and stick it on tempered Masonite, 1/16-inch hobby-shop plywood, or anything handy that is stable and reasonably tough. I use tempered Masonite because it has both of those qualities and is readily available at my local lumberyard.

Now saw the profile pattern right to the line and, with sandpaper glued to a flexible batten, sand the edges fair.

Lay the hull profile pattern on your block. Eyeball it to ensure it has room all around. To level the pattern on the plug, position it so the forward end of the bottom is ¾ inch up from the bottom of the block and the after end is 11/16 inch up. (See Figure 3-2.)

With the profile pattern still in place, mark the stations: a pencil dot, top and bottom of the hull, will do. Mark around the pattern, tracing its shape on the block. Trace the shape on the other side of the block, following the same procedure for the Friendship clam dory in Chapter 2.

Saw Out the Profile

Lay the block on the table of your bandsaw with one side of the profile up, the other down. Set the bandsaw to cut 1 degree off plumb, so when you make the sheer and bottom cuts you will clear the lines underneath that cannot be seen. You must do this, because even if you sit on the right hand of God, you are extremely unlikely to hit the underneath lines fair and square with a straight up-and-down cut. Sure, intentionally cutting away from the underneath lines will leave a little more wood to

3-1 A table saw with the fence and miter gauge removed makes the perfect flat surface for gluing up the block of wood used for the plug. Don't forget to put a sheet of wax paper under the laminations, or you will have a most interesting table saw with a block of wood glued to it.

3-2 The profile pattern is positioned on the block with the station lines aligned, and the after end 11/16 inch from the bottom edge and the forward end ¾ inch. Two sliding squares are used to reposition the pattern on the other side of the block (see description in Chapter 2).

SHEET TWO

HIGGINS & GIFFORD BANKS DORY
MODEL PATTERNS BY D. PAYSON
SCALE 1" = 1'-0" 1/12 ACTUAL SIZE.
DRAWN BY R. LANE DEC. 1995
SHEET NO. 2

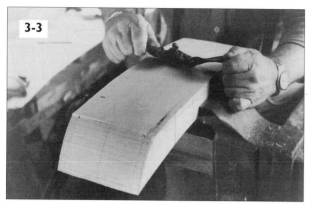

3-3 *After the profile has been sawed out, fair to the lines with a spokeshave and whatever other tool it takes.*

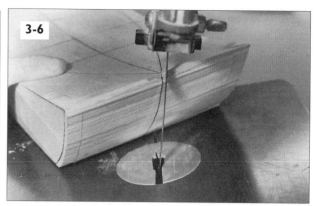

3-6 *With the bandsaw table set at 12 degrees, begin cutting the plan view at the bow, about ⅛ inch off the line.*

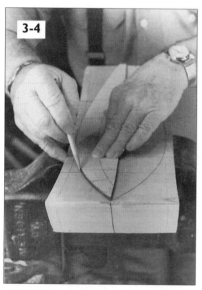

3-4 *The pattern for the plan view, top of the block, shows only half of the territory. Match the edge representing the centerline of the pattern with the centerline of the block, align the station lines, and mark one side. Turn the pattern over and repeat the process for the other side.*

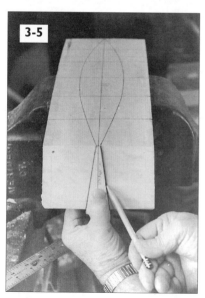

3-5 *The shape of the bottom has been drawn on the bottom of the block, and now the transom is being marked with a pattern.*

take off later, but this is what you want. If you think trimming by hand to the lines later is difficult, consider how difficult it would be to put wood back if you missed those unseen lines.

Cut the sheerline first, and the line of the bottom next. Then saw the ends of the plug along the lines of the transom and the stem. Keep in mind the set of the bandsaw and the whereabouts of the underneath lines. You must preserve those lines.

Fair the Profile

With a spokeshave, a low-angle block plane, files, sandpaper, even a piece of window glass as a scraper — whatever it takes — fair to the lines, straight across the plug from side to side. (See Figure 3-3.) To check the line of the sheer and the rocker (fore-and-aft curve) of the bottom for accuracy, make wooden patterns of those shapes from the plans and try them on the plug.

Plumb and square is what this is all about. Keep your centerline plumb, your station lines square, and the curved lines will take care of themselves.

Establish the Plan View and the Shape of the Bottom

Establish the station lines across the top and bottom of the plug before sawing out the plan view of the plug — the shape of the top, labeled "Sheer Plan" on Sheet Two, and the bottom, labeled "Inside Bottom." Then cut out and mount the patterns for these shapes.

Lay the pattern for the bottom on the plug, aligning it with the stations and the centerline, and trace around it. Do the same with the pattern for the top. (See Figure 3-4.) Bear in mind that the length of the hull you see in plan view is drawn on flat paper, so it doesn't match the length of the curved sheer you see in the profile of the hull. This is a very small difference;

deal with it the same way you did when making the plug for the Friendship clam dory.

With the top and bottom views marked on the plug, you have automatically determined the width of the transom at the top and the width of the extreme after end of bottom. Connect the top and bottom lines on the raked after end of the plug, and you have marked the inside shape of the dory's transom, or use the pattern from Sheet Two. (See Figure 3-5.) Simple isn't it?

Cut the Plan View to Shape

Stay alert. Think about what you are doing as you go. You don't want to saw off one view before you mark the station lines for the next. Sawing out the plug is really quite straightforward, but it is involved enough to demand that you stay awake.

After this much work you don't want to saw inboard of the chine line, the edge where the sides and the bottom meet. To prevent this from happening, set the plug on the table of the bandsaw with the bottom down and the top up, with the centerline of the bow facing the edge of the blade. (See Figure 3-6.) Tilt the table of the bandsaw so when you cut around the plan view the blade will be well clear of the chine line. I have found that setting the table at 12 degrees works for me when I start the cut ⅛ inch outside the top line, right at the stem. (See Figures 3-7 and 3-8.)

If you are unsure about your bandsaw skills even when making a minimum bevel cut, then set your table flat, with no tilt, and simply saw around the top of the plug as close to the line as you trust yourself. You can't go wrong using this approach. All it means is that you will have more wood to remove by hand, but on a plug this small it is no big deal.

Trim and Fair the Sides

With both sides of the plug sawed as close to the lines as you can, trim the sides so they are straight from the sheer to the chine and run in a fair curve from the bow to the stern. (See Figure 3-9.) To protect the plug while you work, sandwich it with a couple of pieces of scrap wood and hold it in a vise. Use a drawknife to remove much of the excess quickly, then switch to a low-angle block plane, a spokeshave, and a flat file.

When you are down to the nitty-gritty, use the flat side of your block plane to test that you have the sides straight from the sheer to the chine. (Figure 3-10.) But note that, since the stem is rounded in profile, the plug naturally rounds slightly between the stem and Station 1. There should be no flatness in that section; rather, it should be slightly convex. Don't fight it; let it fair out.

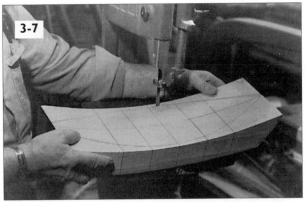

3-7 *Stay alert and follow the old boatbuilder's adage: Leave the line. If you wander inside the line, you will have ruined the plan view.*

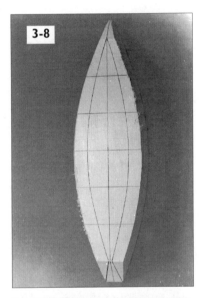

3-8 *As this view of the bottom of the plug shows, a bandsaw setting of 12 degrees takes off some of the bevel of the sides, but not all. This leaves plenty of margin for error.*

3-9 *Take down the excess wood along the sides with a sharp drawknife. Watch the grain and go with it.*

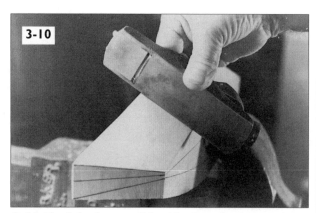

3-10 *Check for flatness of the sides from the sheer to the chine with the side of a plane.*

Finish the plug with 60-grit sandpaper, 180-grit, then 220-grit or finer. Glue a piece of wood to the top of the plug as a handle for holding it in a vise.

Does the plug meet your expectations? If it doesn't, don't worry. Make another. It will be a good experience. Saw the rejected plug right down the centerline, mount the halves on backboards, and you will have two lovely half models.

THE STEM

The plug is prepared for the stem the same way as for the Friendship clam dory. Mark the stem profile on the plug, and cut down and across the plug's stem area until the width at the flat is the same as the width of the stem. (See the plan view on Sheet One, and Figure 3-11.) When this is done it automatically shows how deep to cut the plug for a pocket to receive the stem and the amount to be left outside for beveling. A razor saw and a

3-11 *Cut back and flatten the stem area to make the width of the flat equal to the width of the stem, taking care to maintain the profile of the stem.*

³⁄₁₆-inch chisel perform this job nicely. Keep in mind that the stem pocket must be cut plumb with the centerline and the correct profile must be maintained.

Make the stem according to the pattern shown in the upper right corner of Sheet Two, fit it in the plug's stem pocket, mark a centerline on it, and bevel it fair with the sides of the plug to accept the planking.

Remove the stem, then seal the plug with shellac, sand it lightly, and spray with silicone to prevent glue from sticking to it.

From here on, you can use the patterns shown on Sheet Two, or you can make and fit your own. I will describe how to do the latter as we proceed.

THE TRANSOM

Determining the shape of the transom without using a pattern is very easy. Place a piece of wood a scale inch thick on the transom end of the plug and trace around it. Make the top of the transom higher than indicated, however — about ⅜ inch or so — so you will have room to maneuver when you cut the crown and the reverse bevel. You will be able to create a shape that your eye tells you is right. Without that excess, you might have to go with a flatter crown, perhaps not at all what you had in mind.

Saw the transom to shape (see Figure 3-12), position it on the plug, pin it there, and bevel the edges so they fair into the sides of the plug. Don't make those beveled edges flush with the sides, however; leave them slightly proud, so the ends of the planks land on the edges of the transom, not on the plug.

THE BOTTOM

The bottom, too, is a scale inch thick and is made from a piece of stock 2⅞ inches wide by 15½ inches in

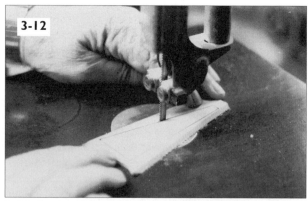

3-12 *Cutting the transom on a bandsaw. The shape of the transom can be taken directly from the plug, or the pattern on Sheet Two can be used. Whatever the method, add a little to the top for the crown and the reverse bevel.*

length. Lay the stock on the bottom of the plug, tape it so it can't move, and trace out the shape. Mark an X on the after end, so you won't confuse it with the forward end later. Set your bandsaw at 15 degrees and saw out the bottom, leaving the line by $\frac{1}{32}$ inch or so.

A nice touch is to scribe caulking seams along the bottom to simulate individual planks. Five planks looks about right. (Remember, the bottom planks of dories run longitudinally, not athwartships.) Do your scribing with a needle stuck in a wooden handle.

Pin the bottom in place on the plug, and trim and fair the edges. As with the transom, leave the edges a whisker proud of the plug. Mark the position of Station 3 on the outside edge of the bottom, so you can relocate the bottom exactly on the plug when you put it back. (See Figure 3-13.)

Mark each frame station on the inside bottom; a dot with a sharp pencil is all you need. Connect the dots across the panel, and you will know precisely where the frames go.

Put a drop of glue on the bottom of the stem, lay the bottom planking on the plug, and pin and tape it down. (See Figure 3-14.) Don't bother gluing the bottom planking to the bottom edge of the transom, because there isn't enough surface for good bonding strength.

THE PLANKING

As mentioned earlier, we are planking this model with 3 strakes to the side. Later, when you have more experience, you might consider building another according to the specifications of the original dory shown on Sheet One.

For working on the planking, make up a planking bench as described in Chapter 2 for the Friendship clam dory.

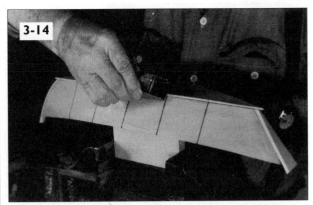

3-14 *The stem has been positioned in the stem pocket, the transom has been pinned in place, and the bottom has been fastened down with a drop of glue at the stem and with pins elsewhere. Now is the time to finish the beveling of the edges of the bottom so they fair into the sides of the plug and the edges of the transom and stem.*

The Garboard

Fitting the garboard on this dory is extremely easy — much easier than for the Friendship clam dory — because the top edge of the plank is straight, not curved. Why? The building of Banks dories was a competitive business, and every builder was looking for the fastest, the easiest, and the best ways to make a buck. One of these ways was to use straight-edged planks, the shaping and cutting of which reduced construction time.

To fit the garboard, then, all you have to do is spot the heights of the top edge on the stem and the transom, and bend around a straight-edged plank wide enough to touch those heights, with enough width left over to mark the shape of the bottom edge at the chine. (See Figure 3-15.)

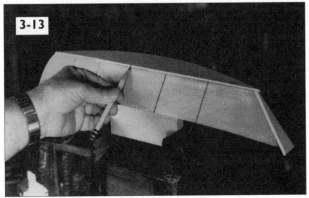

3-13 *Mark the edge of the bottom at Station 3 to allow precise positioning when the bottom is finally fastened down.*

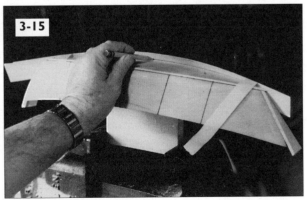

3-15 *Without using the pattern, finding the bottom edge of the garboard is simplicity itself. Position a straight-edged piece of stock at the marks for the top of the garboard and trace off the bottom at the chine.*

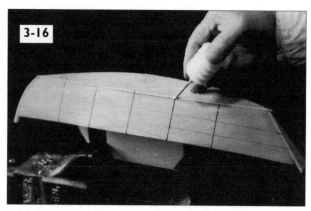

3-16 *To hang the garboard, apply a bead of glue along the edges of the bottom planking, the stem, and the transom. The glue applicator I'm using here, available from model tool suppliers, is a handy little gadget as it allows you to put the glue exactly where you want it. It comes with a cap that doesn't work — it allows the glue in the applicator to dry up over time — so you might as well throw it away. Replace it with a thin plug made from a nail or wire that can be pushed into the applicator's aperture.*

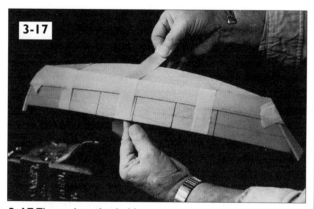

3-17 *The garboard is held it position while the glue dries with strategically placed masking tape. The plank should bear tightly everywhere: at the chine, the stem, the transom, and along the side of the plug.*

How did I decide how high I wanted the ends of the garboard to lie? Look at the dory profile on Sheet One. Note that the forward end runs more than halfway up the stem, which means that the builders back in the 1880s used a plank that was at least 18 inches wide to do the job. That's a rather wide plank to my taste. I also didn't like the looks of such a high end. I therefore lowered the forward end about 3 inches, real measure, and kept the after end at the height shown. This put the after end lower than the forward end, which, in my opinion, is as it should be for looks.

So for the model I spotted these heights and cut a plank a scale 20 inches long by 1⁵⁄₁₆ inches wide by a strong ¹⁄₃₂ inch thick. (While you are at it, cut all the model planking stock to these dimensions.) The plank thickness on the full-size dory is ⁵⁄₁₆ inch; a strong ¹⁄₃₂ inch for the model is pretty close. Keep in mind that the thinner the planking, the less beveling you will have to do, so it is advantageous to be on the thin side.

Use the patterns on Sheet Two to locate and mark the planking heights. Lay the garboard pattern on the plug with its bottom edge aligned with the chine of the plug. Hold the patterns in place while marking with masking tape and pins.

When sawing out the garboard, leave ⅛ inch excess at the ends and ¹⁄₁₆ inch or more at the bottom edge. Make a pair exactly alike.

Before the garboard is hung, the top edge must be beveled to receive the plank above it. The procedure here is the same as for the Friendship clam dory, so follow the instructions in Chapter 2. The width of the lap on the full-size Banks dory is 1³⁄₈ inches, but I feel that 1⅛ inch will serve, which translates to about ⅛ inch on the model. The angle of the bevel should be about 10 degrees; as on the Friendship, increase the angle at the gains, tapering down to a featheredge.

Re-mark the line defining the width of the lap — you'll need that line for reference when hanging the next plank — then give the garboard a dry run. Put it in place and check that there is ample wood left at the ends and along the bottom, and that the top of the garboard is on the height marks, and make a relocating mark on the garboard and bottom planking. Now remove the garboard and prepare for final hanging.

As with the Friendship clam dory, apply a light coat of Franklin Titebond glue along the edge of the bottom planking (see Figure 3-16) and along the stem and transom, align the garboard with the relocating mark and press it flat against the plug amidships, and let the ends flow around to the marked heights of the top edge. In final adjustment the plank must bear flat against the plug everywhere it touches. Hold it there, paying special attention to the ends, with strips of ¾-inch masking tape until the glue dries. (See Figure 3-17.) Trim the ends of the plank flush with the stem and the transom (see Figure 3-18), and then hang the other garboard.

The Remaining Planks

Plank 2, the one between the garboard and the sheerstrake, is next. Note that the top edge of this plank is straight, but the bottom edge of this plank is curved, which may seem strange to you as the top of the garboard is straight. The curvature is caused by twist in the area of the hull where Plank 2 is hung.

The procedure here is the same as for the Friendship clam dory. Both edges of the plank must be beveled — the bottom edge to match the top of the garboard, and the top edge to catch the lap of the sheerstrake. Before you start beveling, fix in your mind which side of the plank must be beveled, and which end of the plank faces forward and which faces aft. Once you have it figured out, make a light reference mark on the plank to help you remember.

It is very easy to make a mess of this, to make two planks alike instead of a mirror-image pair. How do I know?

Mr. Murphy strikes again.

The sheerstrake is the next to go on. Note that both edges are straight, but they are not parallel. The bottom edge of the plank is beveled to match the bevel on the top edge of Plank 2. The top edge is not beveled, but excess wood is left on it to stand proud of the top of the plug by about ⅛ inch. This allows room to maneuver when marking and cutting the sheer.

TRIM THE HULL

Before removing the planked hull from the plug, mark the line of the sheer along the top of the plug onto the inside of the sheer plank (see Figure 3-19). Also, mark the location of the tops of the frames on the inside of the sheer plank. To do this simply make a dot with a pencil point at each frame station.

Sand the ends of the planking flush to the stem and the transom, and pull the pins holding the dory to the plug. Close up the holes made by the pins by rubbing across the grain with the end of a stick wet with water.

Plane the edges of the garboard flush to the bottom planking (see Figure 3-20), sand the bottom, and then pull the hull free from the plug. If it doesn't come off readily, thunk the top of the transom lightly; this should free it. So far I have not had one model that couldn't be freed. The best insurance? Accurately placed glue sparingly applied, and silicone spray.

With the hull off the plug, connect the frame tops with the station lines running across the inside of the bottom planking. Do this before cutting the top of the sheerstrake to the line, or you are liable to lose your top-of-frame dots in the cutting. If you plan to finish the inside of your dory bright, then mark these reference lines lightly so they can be erased later.

Note on the plans that there is a pair of frames near the bow that tilt forward, and another pair near the

3-18 *Trim the ends of the garboard at the stem and the transom with a single-edge razor blade.*

3-19 *Before removing the hull from the plug, use the plug to mark the top of the sheerline on the inside of the sheerstrakes and the positions of the top of the frames.*

3-20 *Plane the edges of the garboard to lie flush with the bottom. The block on top of the plug is there to act as a grip when clamping the setup in a vise.*

3-21 *Whenever I begin to doubt that there is more than one way to build and finish off a dory, I stroll out in my field and take a look at the nest of dead dories lying there. Here's one, with another just barely visible inside, that has quite interesting planking lines, to say the least.*

3-22 *The cross spalls are in, the stern knee and arch board are fitted, and the holes for the beckets have been drilled.*

stern that tilt aft. Neither pair lies on a station line. These are known as cant frames and will be marked for and fitted in later.

It is safe now to cut the excess wood from the sheer, right down to the line. A razor blade is excellent for roughing it out, but be mindful of the grain. When close to the line switch to a modeler's plane, then a sanding batten.

Now, to spread the sides to the proper width, cut three cross spalls for Stations 1, 3, and 5. Follow the procedure as in Chapter 2 for the Friendship clam dory, including notching the ends to make room for the gunwale. Note that patterns for these cross spalls are provided in the bottom right corner of Sheet Two.

This is a good time to decide how you are going to paint this dory. Will you be painting it inside and out, or leaving it clear on the inside and painting the outside?

You must take precautions against glue stains if you will be using a clear finish. In the event, give the dory a coat of shellac thinned 50-50 with alcohol solvent. The shellac, and careful application of glue, will keep staining to a minimum.

FINISH OFF THE HULL

As mentioned previously, there are many ways to finish off a dory, and all of them are okay. Some dories have no rubrails, some have no caprails, some have open gunwales — take your pick. Whatever your skill and patience allow is the way to go. (See Figure 3-21.)

I'll show you my way. It works, it looks good, it is traditional, and it dresses up the dory, which I especially like. In modelmaking details and workmanship make the model.

The Transom

Fit the stern knee and the arch board, patterns for which are given in the upper left corner of Sheet Two. Note that the top of the arch board is beveled to flow into the plank sheer, and the ends are beveled to fit the sides. There's no need to bevel the bottom edge; just round the corner that shows with sandpaper.

Drill the becket holes straight through the arch board and the transom. (See Figure 3-22.) To make sure they are positioned correctly inside and out — that is, they must be as equally spaced and aligned on the outside of the transom as they are on the inside — you might make a test run with a very fine needle, then follow with a drill.

Gunwales

Each gunwale is installed in two pieces laminated together. I tried one piece, but had no luck sawing out a shape that would work. Not that it can't be done, but doing it requires more work and skill than the result is worth.

These pieces for the full-size boat are 20 feet long by 2 inches wide by ⅝ inch thick and are scaled down for the model. Two laminated together equal the molded depth of the top of the frames, just what we need. They are also the right size for the rubrails, but only one per side of the boat. You therefore might as well mill out 6 pieces at the same time — 4 for the gunwales, 2 for the rubrails.

Before you install the gunwales, make each one a little more graceful by tapering the ends slightly (in profile and plan view). Just a few swipes of a modeler's plane does this quickly.

The after end of the gunwale is beveled to fit against

the arch board and should be fitted first. To make the fit at the stem, with a fine chisel cut down the top of the stem, just aft of the forward face, for a notch to accept the forward end of the gunwale. No need to be fussy here, as the caprail will cover this area.

Use instant glue for gluing in the gunwales. Clamp one of the pieces in place, give it a shot of glue along the seam, put in its mate, and apply another shot of glue. (See Figure 3-23.) Do the same on the other side of the boat.

You will notice that the inside edges of the gunwales are a bit high near the stem — too high to fair in nicely with the breasthook, which will be going in next — so sand the top inboard edges down a bit.

Breasthook

The breasthook should be made slightly thicker than indicated in the plans so the top surface can be crowned. Bevel the side edges so the piece will slip down in place between the gunwales. Glue it there. After the glue has dried, crown the top.

Caprails

The caprails cover the gunwales and are sawn to shape according to the pattern on Sheet Two. (See Figure 3-24.)

Each caprail passes over the transom and is cut off flush with the outside face of it. (See Figure 3-25.) With a razor blade cut a notch in the upper corner of the transom that is wide enough to accept the width of the caprail. The after end of the caprail can be either full width or tapered a little for improved looks.

To fit the forward end of the caprails, lay each piece in place and, with a razor blade or a razor saw, cut matching miters aligned with the centerline of the stem.

Clamp the caprails in position, then run instant glue down the joints.

False Stem

The false stem can be sawn to shape according to the pattern in the upper right corner of Sheet Two, or it can be sawn as a straight stick and bent in place over the stem. If you have a hot stovepipe in your shop, bend it over that; otherwise, soak the outside of the bend.

The false stem is applied to the stem square edged, then a centerline is scribed on it and the piece is faired to the planking. Franklin Titebond works well for this job.

Top of the Transom

While you wait for the glue for the false stem to dry, round the top of the transom. Don't be afraid to do this by eye. Sketch a curve on both sides of the transom that

3-23 *The gunwales are laminated in place in two pieces. Here, instead of my fancy modeler's clamps, I'm using clothespins to hold the pieces while I run instant glue into the joints.*

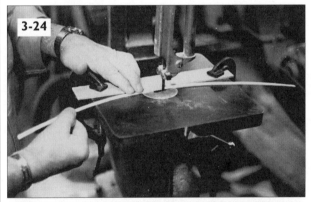

3-24 *You can saw out the caprails freehand on a bandsaw, but I don't recommend that. Clamp a thin piece of stock onto the table and use it as a fence.*

3-25 *I'm using the modeler's clamps to hold the caprail in place.*

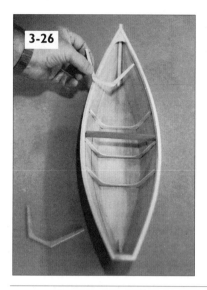

3-26 *Full-size dory frames are made in three pieces, but a single piece is fine for a model. Fit and fasten the middle frames first, then those in the ends.*

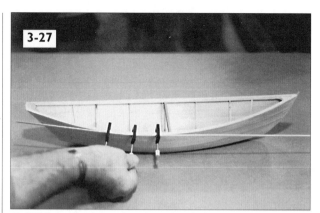

3-27 *The rubrails can be aligned with the top or the bottom of the caprail — take your pick. As with the gunwales, clamp the rubrails in place, starting from the middle and going to the ends, and then run instant glue into the joints.*

blends in with the caprails. If you don't trust your sketching ability, use a compass or a circle template.

Whittle down to your line, and fair the curve with sandpaper, blending the top surface of the transom into the top surface of the caprails. Then, with a ⅛-inch rattail file, shape the sculling notch.

Frames and Cleats

The frames in the full-size dory are sided 1 inch and are constructed of three pieces, with metal clips reinforcing the joints. I make the frames all in one piece for my models. Basswood is a good choice for them, because there's little worry about breakage at the cross-grain. Sometimes I use metal clips made from scrap aluminum printing plates to trick the eye into thinking there are joints in the corners. Sometimes, because 20 clips are required, and it's a chore to make them, I don't. I find it interesting that no one has commented either way; this is because the irons hardly show in the model, especially if it is painted.

Note that on Sheet One the hull profile shows Frames 1 and 2 positioned forward of the station marks; Frames 3, 4, and 5 are aft of the marks.

Fit and position Frame 3 first, as it doesn't require beveling where it lies against the sides of the hull. Then go on to Frames 2 and 4, and follow with Frames 1 and 5, all of which must be beveled. (See Figure 3-26.) Don't forget to knock off the corners of the frames at the chine to make limber holes. Leave the Station 3 cross spall where it is until all the frames and thwarts have been positioned and glued.

Now fit the bottom cleats, the dimensions and positions of which are shown on Sheet Two. Note that the ends must be kept back from the garboards to provide for waterways.

The cant frames in the full-size dory are 1 inch by 2 inches. Their positioning is indicated on the hull-profile pattern on Sheet Two. To get it right, measure forward, top and bottom, from Frame 1 and aft from Frame 5. Note that they must be beveled at the bottom to follow the line of the chine.

Rubrails

Check that the stem and caprails are faired to the planking, so the rubrails will lie snugly against the sides.

Taper the ends of rubrails both in profile and plan view; this is one of those finer touches that adds to the final good looks of the boat.

There are two ways to position the rubrails: one with their top surface flush with the top of the caprails, the other flush with the bottom of the caprails. I use the first method, which is the one used by the builder of the fleet of dead seine dories that have taken up permanent residence in my pasture. (See Figure 3-27.) As I said before, there are many ways of finishing off these dories. You won't be faulted for your choice, or the reasons for it.

Trim the ends of the rubrails flush to the transom and the stem, cut the false stemhead flush with the breasthook and the rubrails, and round off the ends and the edges of the rubrails.

Painter Holes

Drilling for the painter holes sounds simple, but positioning them so they match up on both sides of the bow is not. I've tried it by eye many times and failed as often as not, so now I use the pattern in the upper right corner of Sheet Two. I recommend that you do, too.

3-28 *Deep-throated clamps are required to hold the thwart risers in place while they are glued. Note that everything else has been installed: frames, cleats, gunwales, caprails... the works.*

Risers and Thwarts

Note on Sheet One that in the original full-size dory the risers, which support the thwarts, follow the curve of the sheer. The original also has three thwarts notched into Frames 2, 3, and 4, and two more at the ends of the boat. The ends of the latter appear to be sitting on nothing, but rather to be jammed into the planking. (I'm told they rested on cleats.) For the model, I decided to lengthen the risers, so they can support all the thwarts. I much prefer the looks of this arrangement.

The risers are made according to the pattern on Sheet Two. They go in square-edged; in other words, their tops are not beveled.

The points where the risers cross the frames can be determined from the construction section in the lower left-hand corner of Sheet One. Measure the distance from the top of the caprail to the top of the riser, make a wooden gauge rabbeted to that distance, hang one end of the gauge on the caprail, and mark all five frames, both sides of the boat. (You can use a ruler instead of a gauge, but I find the gauge quicker; besides, used properly, it guarantees accuracy.)

Cross-grain absorbs glue, and there is a lot of cross-grain in the frames where the risers hit them. Therefore, before you put in the risers, it is best to spot-glue each frame at the mark with thicker instant glue, and allow it to soak in and harden. Then you can clamp in your risers and glue them.

Determine the center of a riser and align that center with Frame 3 at the mark. Then position the riser at the marks on the frames and, if you have small clamps with deep jaws, clamp it. (See Figure 3-28.)

I have a boxful of deep-jawed modeling clamps for putting in risers and working in other difficult-to-reach places. You won't find these valuable little items in the run-of-the-mill hobby shop or catalog operation. I bought mine from R. Ullom Co. in Orwell, Vermont. Mr. Ullom used to specialize in clamps and other devices for musical instrument making. His clamps have a movable screw pad to allow clamping on uneven surfaces and are nicely made. Unfortunately, he doesn't make them anymore. Lacking deep-throated clamps you will have to brace or pin the riser to the frame while the glue dries.

With the risers in place, hold them permanently with a shot of thin instant glue at each frame.

The thwarts in the full-size dory are 1 inch thick by 9½ inches. For the model, use the patterns in the lower left-hand corner of Sheet Two.

Fit all the thwarts with their ends loose to the sides, and beveled a bit to hasten the process. Notches to fit over the frames can be sawed quickly with your table saw fitted with a planer blade, because this automatically bevels the inside of the notch where it fits against the frame. For finer fitting of the notch, use a square-edged modeler's file.

Thole Pins

Thole pins or no thole pins? The full-size Banks dory has four sets — that's 16 pins — each pair set 3 inches apart. I don't put them in my models, because it is so easy for someone to break them off in the handling. Furthermore, thole pins look as if they would be easy to make, but they are not. Each one requires a shoulder so it can't fall through the hole bored in the caprail for it.

But if you have to have them, you have to have them. My suggestion is to get your hands on some of those martini sticks used for spearing olives. They should be just the right scale for this dory's thole pins. If not, adjust them until they are.

If you decide to head out to a cocktail lounge to drink martinis for the thole pins, raise a glass in a toast for your dory, because you're almost done.

Final Details

All that remains now are a pair of 8-foot oars, a cradle, a scoop or bailer, and a transom becket. All but the becket have patterns on Sheet Two. Follow the instructions on how to make all these in Chapter 2 on the Friendship clam dory.

PAINT AND VARNISH

My comments in Chapter 2 on painting the Friendship clam dory apply here as well, right down to the choice of color and the application of paint.

If you seek a yachty look, you ought to finish the rubrails bright. But if you do, you should paint the undersides of the rails, as you will get a sharper line. Here's how to do it:

Seal the rubrails with thinned shellac. After the shellac has dried, lay masking tape along the outboard surface of the rails. Paint the outside of the dory, including the under surface of the rails. Remove the masking tape and sand the outboard surface of the rails with 300- to 400-grit paper. This will sharpen up the paint line and remove any paint that may have worked its way under the masking tape. Finally, shoot a little polyurethane spray into a small container, dip a clean rag in it — pantyhose works great — and rub it on the rails.

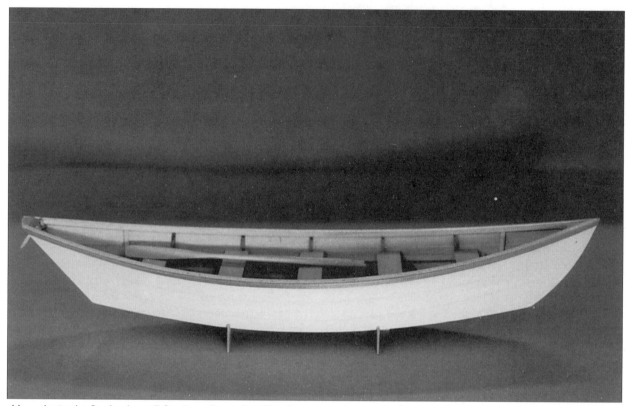

Here she is, the Banks dory all fitted out for a trip of fish. To my eye, the simple elegance of this dory type cannot be topped.

CHAPTER 4

The 12-foot Friendship Dory-Skiff

The prototype for this lovely dory-skiff, or half-dory — a rowboat — evolved many years ago from the Friendship clam dory described in Chapter 2. In the mid-1930s, Carlton Simmons of Friendship modified the design for use with a small outboard motor. He built about 100 boats over a 20-year period, selling them for between 60 to 90 dollars apiece. Most were shipped out of state for use as yacht tenders, camp boats, and livery craft. Some stayed behind in Friendship, however, and a few still survive there. Bob Lane took the lines off one of these, and drew plans for building the full-size dory-skiff and patterns for making a model.

The Friendship dory-skiff has the same round sides, the same general appearance, and the same superb rowing qualities as her close kin, the clam dory. In addition, with her wider transom than that of a traditional dory, she easily carries an outboard motor of 2 or 3 horsepower, the commonly used power of her heyday.

I decided to build a model of this dory-skiff because I liked how she looked. I also did it because I feel that building a model — and drawing up plans, too — of an obscure boat type provides that type with a good chance of surviving. Even as I write this I'm tracking down other boats once common to my section of the coast of Maine, among them the Monhegan skiff, which is still used by fishermen on Monhegan Island, and a small one-man lobsterman's skiff unique to Spruce Head. Oh yes, and an old used-up peapod designed and built many years ago by Alton Whitmore. There is so much to be learned in tracking down these old relics, and it is, indeed, a privilege to record them before they are gone. Too many of these lovely craft are gone

already, but thanks to Bob Lane and his drafting expertise, here's another one to share with you that didn't get away.

The technique of building a model of this boat is the same as for the Friendship clam dory and the Banks dory, so I am not going into detail here. You can be guided by what you learned in the previous chapters. Generally, construction is the same: Build a plug, plank over it, pull the hull off the plug, and finish it. Since the procedure is the same I'll just give you the basics and you do the rest. All the information you need for building the model is right on the plans.

Here's the nuts and bolts of it:

■ Make a plug from 10 pieces of wood ¾ inch by 18 inches by 3¼ inches. Draw the station lines around the plug. Lay the skiff profile pattern on the plug and trace around it.

■ Saw out the profile of the plug. You can use a bandsaw here if it can handle a depth of cut of 8 inches or more.

■ Lay the patterns for the plan views of the top and the bottom of the hull, and the transom, on the plug, aligning the station lines on the patterns with those on the plug. (See Figures 4-1 and 4-2.)

■ Saw the plan view of the plug with the bandsaw table set flat so as not to saw off the wood that will be used to shape the tumblehome — the inward curve of the sides at the after quarters. Shape the sides of the plug using the station templates to control roundness. (See Figures 4-3 and 4-4.)

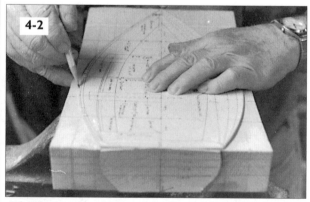

4-1 *The transom and bottom patterns are laid on the block after the profile has been sawn to shape and faired. The transom pattern is aligned with the centerline and waterlines; the bottom with the centerline and the station lines.*

4-2 *The plan view showing the outline of the top of the plug is used to mark that shape on the block. It is aligned with the centerline and the station lines.*

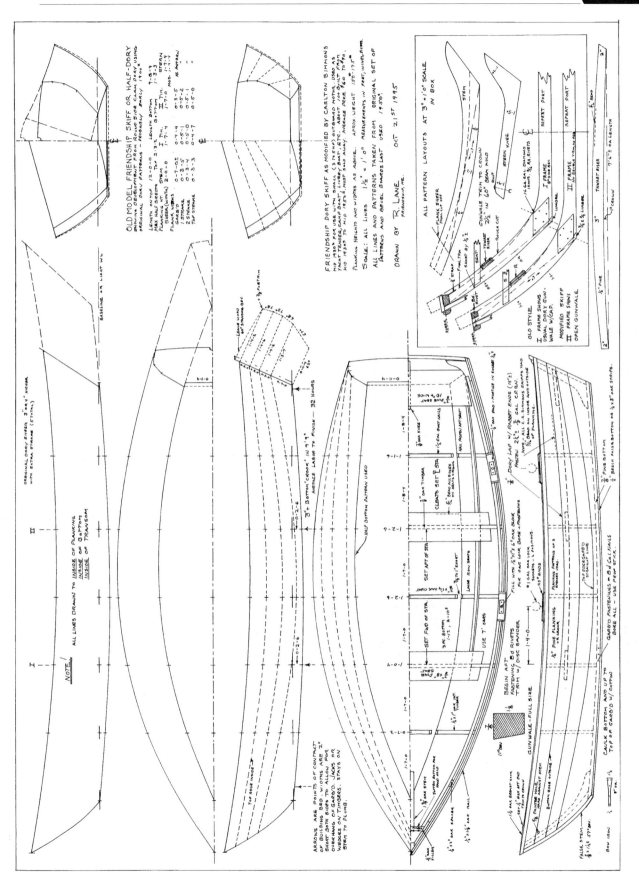

SHEET ONE

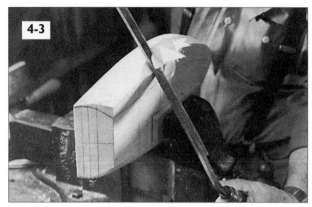

4-3 *Care must be taken when carving the sides of the plug, as, like the Friendship clam dory, they are rounded. In addition, there is a fair amount of tumblehome — inward curvature — in the after quarters and in the top two planks.*

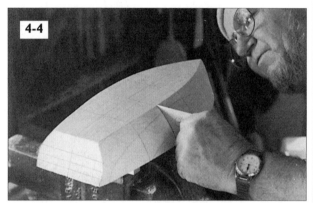

4-4 *You know you have an accurate plug when you offer up the station templates to the sides at the stations and can't see a whisker of daylight. And when the plug is fair between the stations, you know you have an accurate, fair plug.*

4-5 *Here's the garboard plank held above the shape of the lined-off garboard on the plug. Though the plank looks as if it will never fit, it will. When the plank is bent around the plug, the curved edge will appear to have become straight, and the straight edge, curved. That's one of the wonders of boatbuilding that keeps it so interesting.*

■ Draw the planking lines on the plug. Give the plug, except the top, a shot of silicone spray.

■ Make the stem. Trace the profile of the stem on the plug, shape to that line, and cut a pocket for the stem.

■ Mill out the stock for the transom, hold it against the plug, trace off the shape, and saw out the transom. Tape the transom on the plug and, with the transom pattern, mark the shape of the outside surface.

■ Insert the stem in the stem pocket. Lay on the bottom planking, aligning its station lines to that of the plug.

■ Saw out the garboard and bevel the top edge for the lap. On the full-size boat, the planking is ½ inch thick and the width of the lap bevel is ⅞ inch, though more width is okay. (See Figure 4-5.)

■ If you will not be using the plank patterns, before gluing the garboard in place, slip a piece of drafting paper or Mylar under the top edge of the garboard and mark along that edge for the bottom of Plank 2. Take the shape of the top edge of Plank 2 from the planking line on the plug; add to it the width of the lap, ⅞ inch on the full-size boat. Now glue the garboard in place. (See Figure 4-6.)

■ Plank her up, either by using the plank patterns on the plans or by determining the shape of each plank in succession as in the step above.

■ Mark the line of the sheer on the inside of the sheer planks, using the top of the plug as a guide. Spot the tops of the frames. Remove the hull from the plug.

■ Trim the sheer. Give the hull a coat of sealer.

■ Make cross spalls for Stations 1, 3, and 5, notch the ends for the inwales, and install the cross spalls. The cross spalls must remain in place until the risers and seats are in.

■ Make and install the false stem.

■ Make Frames 1 and 2 in one piece, using diamond irons at the simulated joints, and file for the limbers. Insert the frames in the hull and leave the tops high.

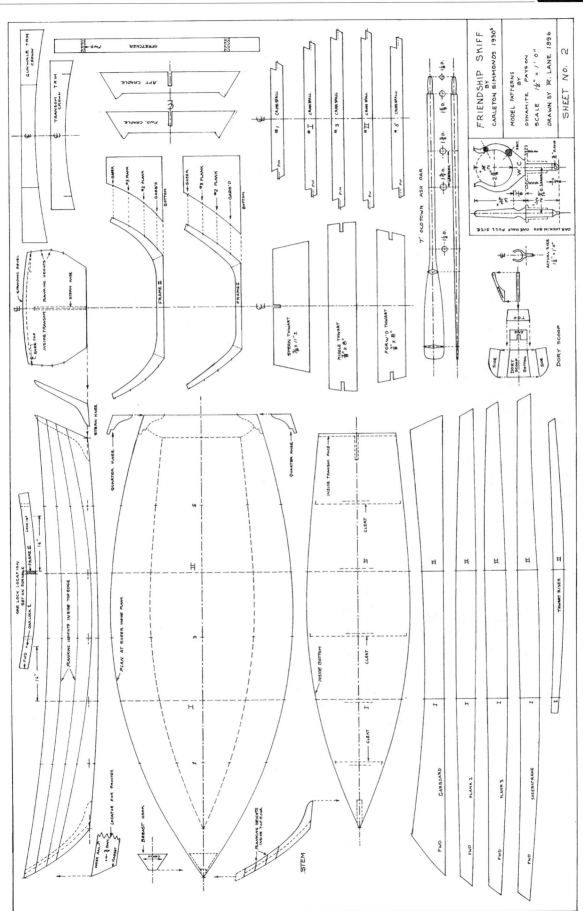

FRIENDSHIP SKIFF
BY
CARLETON SIMMONDS 1930s

MODEL PATTERNS
BY
DYNAMITE PAYSON
SCALE 1½"=1'-0"
DRAWN BY R. LANE 1996

SHEET NO. 2

SHEET TWO

67

4-6 *Sometimes holding down the garboard on the plug while the glue dries takes a lot of masking tape. Tape is cheap. Use however much is required to do the job.*

4-7 *The hull is all planked and framed, with cross spalls keeping the sides spread. Note that the tops of the principal and intermediate frames are high; they will be trimmed to the sheerline later.*

4-8 *The transom crowning board in use. The centerline of the board is aligned with the centerline of the transom. The underside of the board is allowed to rest on the tops of the rubrails, which run out past the transom. Then the transom crown is traced off.*

■ Make and insert the bottom cleats and the intermediate frames. In the full-size boat these are ½ inch by 1 inch. (See Figure 4-7.)

■ Fair the stem into the hull planking. Lay on the false bottom. Make and install the stern knee.

■ Install the fillers on each side of the breasthook (see Sheet 1 of the plans). Make and install the breasthook.

■ Make and install the rubrails; cut the crown, using the gunwale crowning board as a guide.

■ With the transom trim crowning board, mark the crown of the transom. (See Figure 4-8.) Cut to shape, leaving excess stock at the corners. Trim to the line at the corners after the quarter knees and the inwales have been installed.

■ Make the quarter knees according to the pattern. Lay the gunwale crowning board across the gunwales and against the inboard face of the transom, and bring the tops of the quarter knees up to the crowning board. Glue the knees to the transom and the planking.

■ Place a filler block, ½ inch thick on the full-size boat, halfway between the after end of the breasthook filler and the first intermediate frame. This provides a backing for the inwale.

■ Make the inwales. On the full-size boat they are ⅞ inch by 1⅛ inches and beveled 11 degrees. To bend them in place, wet and pre-bend them around a hot stovepipe. No stovepipe? Soak them for a few minutes in household ammonia.

■ Notch the tops of the frames for the inwales (see Figure 4-9), and fit the inwales for length. Lay the gunwale crowning board across the gunwales and bring the inwales up until they touch the bottom of the board; glue the inwales in this position. Cut the top of the frames flush with the rails and smooth all down.

■ The risers are made square edged; in other words, they are not beveled. To bend them in place, wet and pre-bend them around a hot stovepipe or soak them in ammonia.

■ Use the patterns on Sheet Two to make the thwarts. Note that in the full-size boat the middle and forward thwarts are 8 inches wide and the stern thwart is

10 inches wide. Make the thwarts slightly longer than indicated on the patterns to allow excess for adjustment.

■ The oarlock pads in the full-size boat are ½ inch by 2 inches by 8½ inches. They are slightly curved to the gunwales, their ends are cut to a 45-degree bevel, and they are bored for the oarlock shafts with a ⁵⁄₆₄-inch drill. A filler, ½ inch by ⅞ inch, is fitted between each inwale and gunwale under the pads to act as a backer.

■ Paint and/or varnish the boat to taste. My favorite color scheme is a bright finish inside and white paint on the outside, with the gunwales finished bright.

■ Using the patterns on Sheet Two, make a pair of oars and a scoop, or bailer. Seven-foot oars are about right for the full-size skiff. They can be left without protection from chafe on the looms or served with fine 3-strand nylon.

So that's about it for this dory-building operation. If you've been reading through this trying to decide whether to build one for yourself or not, wondering whether you have the skills to do it or not, jump out of that chair and get started. Don't think about it any more. Don't procrastinate. Don't get wishy-washy. Get started. That's the way I did it.

I never spent a day of my life working in a boatyard. I never had a teacher. I never took a boatbuilding course. But I learned how to build and repair full-size boats.

I remember getting an order from designer Phil Bolger to build his 31-foot Folding Schooner. I vividly remember being thoroughly intimidated by all the rigging I was supposed to know all about and didn't. I didn't

4-9 *The tops of the frames are notched for the inwale. The saw I'm using here is a piece of razor-saw blade inserted in a slot at the end of a stick and glued. You can make all sorts of custom modeling tools like this with pieces of saws and razor blades.*

have the slightest idea what the difference was between a peak halyard and a backstay. Yet once I separated out the individual tasks from the larger task — yes, I can build the hull; yes, I can build the masts; yes, I can make up the rigging — I was on my way.

The same can be said about modelmaking. I started from scratch, and so can you.

If after reading all these instructions, you have determined that you will be lucky to build the block for making the plug, and only the block, then go ahead and make it. The start is what counts.

And don't be afraid to make mistakes. Even designer Phil Bolger, who I have worked with for years, admits having made some. He passes them off this way: "The gods are said to get angry if you make no mistakes."

The Friendship dory-skiff, as her name implies, is a skiff derived from a dory and built using the same techniques as traditional dory construction.

CHAPTER 5
A Case For Your Model

A model boat takes on a magical look when displayed in a case. It also stays dust-free, and dust is the enemy of scale models. There are many types of case, but my choice has always been a clear plastic one without wooden or metal corners that can obscure the model inside. The top, sides, and ends are plastic, the bottom is wood.

You can work out the proportions for a case that suits your eye. As an example, for the lovely Banks dory, I made a case 21½ inches long, 6 inches high, and 7 inches wide. I used acrylic window glazing and was able to knock it out in a few hours.

There are many brands of this sheet acrylic, but I use Plexiglas. It comes with a tough protective layer of paper on each side that takes a pencil line and stays in place until it is removed. Some other brands are covered with thin transparent plastic that won't take a pencil line and tends to pull free when you least want it to.

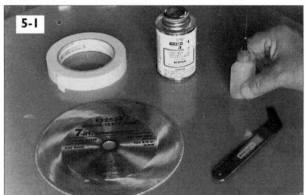

5-1 *The tools of the model case builder: masking tape, acrylic bonding liquid, applicator bottle, cutting tool, fine-toothed saw blade.*

5-2 *I saw my Plexiglas outside, because it creates fumes I'd rather not breathe. I also leave the protective paper on while I cut it.*

Buy your sheet acrylic at a glass center if you can, as their prices tend to be lower than at a hardware store. As of this writing, a 4-foot by 8-foot sheet of Plexiglas is about 50 dollars. Custom cutting, if you have it done for you, will add to the cost, as will a cutting tool if you were to go that route. In addition, figure 10 dollars or so for a bonding liquid applicator and the special bonding liquid itself, both of which will be sold at the same place you buy the Plexiglas. (See Figure 5-1.)

CUTTING THE PLEXIGLAS

I bought a special cutting tool but never use it. Why? I discovered I can cut Plexiglas easier and faster with my Porter Cable hand circular saw with a hollow-ground planer blade or, better yet, a fine-toothed hollow-ground blade with 200 teeth. As this material gives off fumes when cut with a saw, I do my cutting outdoors. I also leave the protective paper on while I saw, and set the depth of the blade so it just goes through the glass and no more. (See Figure 5-2.)

Be careful and precise when laying out your Plexiglas for cutting. The length of the sides and the top will be the same. The width of the ends must be narrower than the width of the top (by two thicknesses of Plexiglas), because the sides will be bonded to them. Make a sketch to clarify in your mind the dimensions of the pieces and what has to be done when they are assembled. If you become confused, make a little model of the case with cardboard and tape.

If you are in doubt about the preciseness of your measuring, it is best to make the ends narrower, as you can always take a dite off the top with your table saw but you sure can't put it back on. Such a cut on your table saw must be absolutely square, so check the accuracy of the table fence and the miter gauge. If they're off, adjust them until they're on. (See Figure 5-3.)

Once the pieces have been cut out, sand the edges with, in succession, 60-, 100-, and 320-grit sandpaper. The final sanding with 320-grit will leave the edges so smooth that when all the pieces are bonded together the edges will appear clear. If the edges are not sanded properly, the edges will have a dull or matte appearance when they are bonded.

ASSEMBLING THE PIECES

Assemble the pieces on a flat, level surface — anything that's not wobbly.

My first attempt at making a Plexiglas case was a bit frustrating, because the instructions that came with the bonding liquid neglected to say whether the joint to be bonded should be vertical or horizontal during application. I tried doing it with the joints horizontal and made a mess of the job. The proper way, as it turns out, is to apply the bonding liquid to vertical joints. The lack of a simple instruction that said "keep joints vertical" caused a lot of extra work and frustration.

Keep the protective paper on the Plexiglas while bonding, so any stray drops of liquid won't splash where they are not wanted, but expose the edges before applying the liquid. Do this by pulling the paper an inch or so back from the corners, then inserting a thin piece of scrap wood or plastic between the paper and the glass, and peeling and cutting the paper back about ½ inch all along the two edges to be joined.

Begin by bonding the side pieces to the end piece. Use masking tape to hold the joints together temporarily. They don't have to be humming tight — just make sure the edges are touching. (See Figure 5-4.)

Bond one joint at a time. Bring the corner to be bonded clear of the table top, so any stray drops of liquid will not land on the table. Apply the liquid carefully. It will bond the joint instantly, changing the appearance of the joint as you watch. The joint will cure to its full strength overnight.

Once all four corner joints have been bonded, set the case on one end, put the top piece in position, and secure it temporarily with masking tape. (See Figure 5-5.) Apply the bonding liquid near the top of one corner; it will travel on its own down the joint to the bottom. Do not overload with liquid, or a puddle will form at the bottom of the joint.

Plexiglas and other acrylics are loaded with static electricity, and sometimes a bit of the liquid will fly off and stick to exposed plastic. If this happens, don't try to wipe it off, as it will only smear the surface and you will end up with a foggy mess. Leave the liquid alone, and it will dry as transparent as the Plexiglas itself.

Once everything is bonded, you can remove the protective paper.

The best acrylic cleaner and polisher I have tried is Novus, which is available from automotive suppliers and comes in two different bottles. Novus #1 cleans, shines, and protects. It is also an antistatic dust repellent for use on all plastic surfaces. Novus #2 is a polish that removes fine scratches and restores the original appearance to plastics.

THE BASE

The base configuration I prefer is a ¾-inch-thick piece of wood rabbeted all around, forming a lip on which the bottom edge of the plastic case rests. I cut the rabbet so the lip is flared 15 degrees. (See Figure 5-6.)

Even though the base of a case looks simple to make,

5-3 Model cases must be plumb and square, and lengths and widths must be right on the money, so perfectly accurate cuts are a must. If you use a table saw, make sure beforehand that the fence and the miter gauge are square to the table.

5-4 A corner to be bonded is aligned so the joint is off the table; any excess bonding liquid will fall to the floor, not the table. Masking tape holds the joint until the bonding liquid takes over. In the text, I recommend leaving the protective paper on at this stage, pulling back only a narrow band at the joint. I removed all the paper for the purposes of photography.

it requires careful finishing so it will look as good as your model. If you use mahogany, Spanish cedar, or oak, the grain must be filled or you won't be able to achieve the beautiful finish you seek. Filler, which can be obtained at your hardware store, should be the consistency of heavy cream and should be applied sparingly across the grain. Too much filler is liable to cause the base to warp.

The safest way to avoid warping and twisting is to do the same thing to both sides of the base, the top and the bottom. In other words, if you're using filler, apply it to the bottom, too, even though no one will ever see that side. The same applies to stains, sealers, varnishes — whatever you use.

5-5 *When bonding acrylic, the secret is to apply the liquid to the top of vertical joints and allow it to run down of its own accord.*

5-6 *The base board is rabbeted around the edges to take the Plexiglas cover. If you are using an open-grain wood, such as mahogany or oak, you should treat the wood with a filler before applying the final finish.*

If the filler is too thick, thin it a little with turpentine. To hasten drying, give it a shot of Japan drier. Allow the filler to dry overnight.

Sand the base and apply the finish coats. I use shellac, because it dries faster than varnish. Then I sand the shellac lightly and give it a coat of Minwax fast-drying polyurethane from a spray can. This will knock out any shiny spots and leave a dull sheen.

So there you have it. A nice little case for a nice little model. Don't be timid about giving it a try. If I can do it, you can do it.

Have fun!

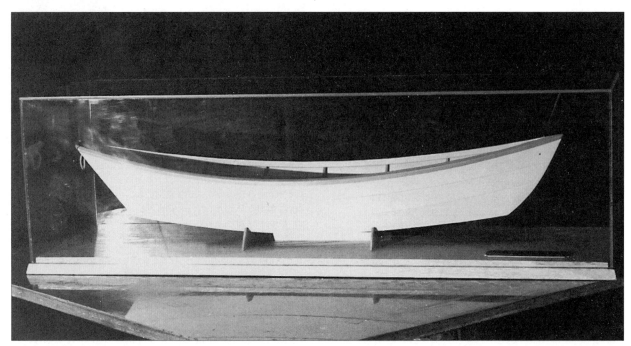

A Banks dory in her own custom case. Though there are any number of ways to build a case, I prefer this method, as it doesn't require corner posts, which can obstruct the view of what's inside.

CHAPTER 6

Modeling Tips

Here are a few random tips and wrinkles I've picked up over the years. Some I learned the hard way, from experience. Others come from modelmakers who have shared their own experience with me.

■ If you don't have an architect's scale rule, buy one and learn how to use it. Get one from an art or drafting supply shop.

■ In the final stages of working on a model, when protecting surfaces from damage is most important, lay an old towel on your bench and put the model on that.

■ Sandpaper backed by a cone-shaped fid is great for working inside curves of all shapes.

■ Emery boards work well for sanding sharp, crisp corners. Make your own by gluing sandpaper to sticks. A set made of 60-, 100-, and 320-grit is a good all-around choice. Make the sticks 1 inch wide and approximately ⅛ inch thick. You can get nine 1-inch sticks from a standard sheet of sandpaper. Hold the sandpaper on the sticks with spray glue. A quick way to do this is to line up your sticks side by side, give them a shot of spray glue, lay your sheet of sandpaper down, wait for the glue to set up, then cut the sticks apart with a utility knife.

■ Another way to make up sanding sticks is to glue a sheet of sandpaper on one large piece of wood of the desired thickness, then rip the sanding strips on a table saw. Since this is hell on saw teeth, use an old, dull blade.

■ In some situations, a sharp scraper is superior to sandpaper. If you don't have a scraper, use the edge of a piece of glass. When the edge becomes dull, break the glass for a new, sharp edge.

■ There are a lot of bevels in model boat building, just as many as in the full-size variety. In model work, however, a regular sliding bevel tool is too bulky. Make a miniature one by cutting two pieces, 1 or 2 inches long, off an old hacksaw blade, drill a hole in one end of each, and rivet them together — a copper nail, cut off and peened over is all it takes. Peter Spectre made me a fancier version from brass modeling stock, and I use it all the time.

■ You can cut your own veneers with a hollow-ground planer blade that has no set to the teeth. First rip the stock parallel with the grain, then turn the stock so the long grain is flat to the table. Ripping the stock now will create vertical-grain veneers. Do not try to do this with heartwood, as it can have wild, unstable grain and a pulpy center.

■ To save your fingers when resawing very thin stock on a table saw, use a push stick made from a thin dowel topped by a cap-style eraser.

■ If the thought of hand-sharpening a hollow-ground planer saw blade bothers you, buy an inexpensive Sears thin-rim satin-cut veneer saw blade and throw it away when dull.

■ Modelmaking lumber can be planed smooth with the small surface planers available from Ryobi, Delta, and others, but special care must be taken. To prevent these power planers from shredding very thin stock, piggyback the stock on something thicker. I use a piece of dead-flat aluminum plate, ⅜ inch thick, but a wooden board will work even though it isn't as stable as aluminum. To avoid cupping at each end of your stock when it drops down on the back roller, run a piece of scrap wood through the planer first, followed immediately by the critical piece, followed immediately by another scrap piece.

■ Jay Hanna says that if you want to paint close to something — for example, along the sheerstrake, against the gunwale — and your hands shake, use a brush with very long bristles. Hold the brush quite flat and "drag" the paint. The long bristles act like a shock absorber, remaining steady while you shake.

■ A tiny, precise stripe — say, $1/16$ inch or less — can sometimes dress up a model, but painting it is no easy matter. An alternative is to lay a random width of masking tape on wax paper, give the tape a blast of spray paint, or brush on the paint, cut off the stripe you need with a razor blade, and stick it on. The tape is easier to cut if you lay it on a piece of scrap acrylic window glazing (Plexiglas).

■ Make your own thin masking material by stripping it off wider tape with a straightedge and a razor blade on a piece of scrap acrylic window glazing. You might also use another piece of scrap acrylic for a straightedge. As you pick up your piece of narrow tape, give it a pull; this will stretch the tape enough to keep it from curling and sticking back on itself.

■ For a flat finish, BIN, a sealer available in most hardware stores, can be used to seal and paint a model at the same time. The essential ingredients are white shellac, denatured alcohol, and white pigment. Peter Spectre has tinted BIN with pigments of other colors, but he says getting the precise color you want is sometimes dicey. BIN dries quickly — 15 to 20 minutes — so only apply with a brush; with a spray gun it dries somewhat in midair, enough to spoil the bond. Clean your brush in a solution of ammonia and warm water, or use denatured alcohol.

■ Chrome spray paint from an auto supply shop provides an almost perfect simulation of galvanizing on small parts, such as diamond irons or frame clips.

■ Spray painting requires a spray booth if you are to avoid having dangerous paint particles floating through the air. If you don't have a store-bought spray booth, a cardboard carton, or a couple of cartons taped together, will do for small jobs. For large jobs, get a proper spray booth. In any event, wear a mask when spraying. In a pinch, for a quick shot of spray, hold your breath.

■ Lacking rubber gloves when spray painting, in a pinch wrap your hand and arm in a plastic bag, grab ahold of the object to be painted, and let her rip.

■ The tightfitting caps of aerosol spray paint cans often stick. To avoid going crazy with frustration from trying to pull off a balky cap, with a sharp knife trim the plastic lip inside the small inner circle inside the cap. The more you trim, the less the friction and the easier it will be to remove the cap.

■ For filling tiny holes and imperfections, Peter Spectre suggests using an artist's palette knife. These are available in various sizes and configurations, or you can buy a standard, no-frills palette knife and customize the blade with a pair of tinsnips and a file.

■ A piece of a single-edge razor blade makes a great miniature putty knife or a chisel. To customize your own, pry the stiff metal finger guard off the back of the blade, put the blade in a vise, snap off a width to suit, and grind to shape. Be sure to protect your eyes with safety glasses. Cut the finger guard to fit the new width of the blade and bond it onto the back of the blade with glue. Then make a wooden handle, cut a slot in the end, and glue the blade in the slot.

■ Some wooden parts are so small they are most difficult to pick up with your fingers. Spear them instead. Make your own spear by fixing the blunt end of a sharp needle or a common pin in a wooden handle.

■ For laying on a drop of thin cyanoacrylate instant glue, Jay Hanna and Arthur Herrick suggest modifying the eye of a needle. Grind off the top of the eye, leaving a "Y" shape, and jam the sharp end of the needle into a stick for a handle. The "Y" holds a drop of the glue for application.

■ Some of the cyanoacrylate instant glues, particularly the less expensive ones, have a strong odor, make your eyes water, and make you feel as if you are coming down with a cold, sure indications that they are bad for your health. Use them with care and thoroughly ventilate the room you are working in. To be extra careful rig a fan so it blows across your face.

■ Some of the cyanoacrylate instant glues aren't quite "instant." To speed them up, use an instant glue activator, available in hobby shops. It is applied with a spray applicator directly on the joint that has been glued, and the results are exactly what the bottle says: "instant bonding." You can also spray the area to be bonded before the glue is applied. Lay down the glue, put the two pieces together, and whammo!, instant bond.

■ Some glue bottles, even when set upright, pump glue between use, and this glue runs down the side of the bottle, sight unseen. To avoid sticky fingers, wrap a couple layers of masking tape around the bottle and let the overflow soak into the tape.

■ Transfer letters, available from art or drafting supply shops, are useful for putting the name on the transom of your model. These letters come on a sheet. To use, draw a reference line on the hull that corresponds with the top of the name. Cut strips across the transfer sheet, flush with the tops of the letters. Align the top of the strip with your reference line, slide right or left to position the letter, and rub the back of the sheet behind the letter to transfer it to the model. X-Acto makes a special tool with a ball on one end and a flat plastic end on the other for laying down the letters and burnishing them. Transfer letters aren't that expensive; make a few test runs on a piece of scrap wood.

■ James E. Waites says an easy way to transfer patterns to wood is to photocopy the pattern, lay the photocopy face down on the wood, and iron with moderate heat.

■ Walter S. Cluett has this to say about making model sails: "I used cloth from BlueJacket Ship Crafters, their item #1300, 'Silkspan' sailmaking cloth, intended for making furled sails. It is much easier to work with than fine silk or nylon. I made the seams with an iron-on wax hemming tape, which is available backed with paper, or unbacked. I used the backed type, as it was easier to use. I cut the material to shape, attached it to one surface, removed the backing, aligned the joint or fold, and finalized the seam. On the luff and foot of the model sail, I folded in a length of line. I reinforced the corners with additional pieces of sail material applied to each side. This is very simple to do: apply wax to a piece of material of sufficient size, cut to shape, remove the backing, align, and iron."

■ If you can't feed the end of a piece of rigging line through a small eye, put some instant glue on it. After the glue has dried, cut the line end to a taper with a razor blade.

■ Miniature screw and nail heads can be simulated in thin brass or aluminum by indenting the backside with a needle.

■ Size tiny drills, wire, and rigging line with a micrometer.

■ Loren Herrick says you can make a steering compass from "Clear Cushion Feet," which are available by the package from Radio Shack. These soft plastic feet are flat on one side and domed on the other, and therefore magnify anything under them. Find a drawing or clear photo of a compass card, reduce it on a photocopier to the diameter of one of the feet, make a base for the card, stick the card to it, and then lay the cushion foot over it.

■ If you won't be making a case for your model for awhile but still want to keep dust off it, drape it with light sheet plastic.

■ A more substantial dust cover is a rectangular box made with plastic right-angle corners covered with light sheet plastic. These corners are sold by the 4-foot section in most hardware stores. They are intended for protecting wall corners, woodwork, cabinets, etc. Whack off pieces to the lengths you want — four for the uprights, eight for the horizontal pieces — glue them together to create your box, and cover with plastic wrap or sometime similar, held in place with plastic tape.

Sources of Supply
& Glossary of Terms

SOURCES OF SUPPLY

**Scale plans of dories described in this book,
as well as plans for other interesting models**
H. H. Payson & Co.
Pleasant Beach Rd.
So. Thomaston, ME 04858
207-594-7587

**Modeling supplies —
tools and materials of all types**
Micro Mark
340 Snyder Ave.
Berkeley Heights, NJ 07922
800-225-1066

Metal fittings, kits, plans, supplies
BlueJacket Ship Crafters
P.O. Box 425
Stockton Springs, ME 04981
800-448-5567

Brass nameplates and non-rusting pins
Van Dyke Supply Co., Inc.
P.O. Box 278
Woonsocket, SD 57385
605-796-4950

Basswood
A. E. Sampson & Son
P.O. Box 1010
Warren, ME 04864
207-273-4000

Scale-model wood
Northeastern Scale Models, Inc.
P.O. Box 727
Methuen, MA 01844
800-343-2094

Small tools and specialty items
Leichtung Workshops
One Woodworker's Way
Seabrook, NH 03874
800-321-6840

Aft
Toward the stern.

After
Closer to the stern.

Amidships
In the middle portion of a boat. As an adjective, 'midship.

Athwartships
Running across the hull. As an adjective, 'thwartship.

Baseline
A line, usually parallel to the waterline, drawn on boat plans and used as a reference for all vertical measurements when lofting the lines of a hull.

Batten
A thin, flat length of wood that can be sprung through a series of reference points and thereby used to determine and draw a fair curve through the points.

Becket
A rope handle used for lifting a barrel, a lobster crate, or the stern of a dory.

Bevel
An angle cut along the edge of a timber or across its end to produce an exact fit between parts.

Body plan
The lines of a hull, as viewed from the ends, showing cross sections.

Breasthook
A type of knee, triangular in shape, that fits in the bow behind the stem and extends from side to side.

Butt
To join end-to-end or edge-to-edge. As a noun, a strap or block fastened across a joint to hold the two elements together. Also the lower end of a mast.

Buttock lines
Vertical slices running fore and aft through the hull parallel to the centerline. In plan view, they show as straight lines; in profile, they are curved.

Centerline
On boat plans, a line dividing a hull into two identical longitudinal halves. It is used as a base for establishing 'thwartship measurements. Also a vertical line on 'thwartship members used to align them during assembly.

Chine
A lower longitudinal joint where two edges meet in a hull. Most commonly, the joint between the sides and the bottom in a flat- or V-bottomed boat.

Cleat
A fitting to which a line can be made fast. Any short length of small dimensional lumber used for miscellaneous framing needs.

Cross spall
A temporary wooden brace extending across the hull from side to side to maintain shape.

Dory
A flat-bottomed craft with flaring sides and a narrow stern. It is capable of carrying heavy loads, but is very tender when light.

Edge-set
To drive one plank down forcibly to meet the plank below regardless of the fit. Not a recommended procedure when done to the extreme.

Face
The flat, broad surface of a board or timber.

Fair
Descriptive of a line that changes gradually without quick humps, hollows, or flat places, and is pleasing to the eye.

False stem
External fairing piece that overlays the planking joint at the stem and protects the ends of the planking.

Flare
The outward angle of a boat's sides between the waterline and the sheer when viewed in cross section.

Flush
Even or level with; not protruding.

Forefoot
The area of the hull where the bottom of the stem meets the forward end of the keel.

Frame
A 'thwartship member to which planking is fastened.

Freeboard
The height of the sheer above the waterline at any given point along a hull.

Garboard
The lowest plank on the hull. On a dory, the plank next to the bottom.

Gunwale
A longitudinal strengthening strip that runs along the sheer of a hull.

Inboard
Inside of the hull, toward the centerline.

Inwale
Longitudinal member at the inboard edge of the sheer.

Knee
A strengthening member that is fastened to two angled members and distributes stress to both.

Lapstrake
A method of planking in which each strake slightly overlaps the one below it, giving the appearance of clapboarding on a house.

Limber holes
Openings in bulkheads or frames that allow water to move from one section of the hull to another.

Molded and sided
Terms for describing the shape of a member. For example, the sided dimension of a stem is an indication of its thickness; its molded dimension is its width when viewed in profile.

Outboard
Outside the limits of the hull, in a direction away from the centerline.

Painter
A length of rope used to tie a boat to keep it from going adrift.

Pattern
A template defining the shape of a part.

Pre-bore
To bore a hole in wood for a nail or other fastening to be driven into. Pre-boring reduces the danger of breaking out or splitting.

Rake
A departure from vertical of any member of a boat, such as the stern, transom, or mast.

Riser
A longitudinal member inside the hull that serves as a support for the thwarts.

Seam
The joint between two planks or strakes, made watertight by caulking.

Seize
To bind together, or to put a stopper on a line. To wrap the loom of an oar with light line for protection from wearing.

Sheer
The uppermost line of a hull when viewed in profile. Also called the sheerline.

Sheerstrake
The top plank, or strake, on a hull.

Sided and molded
Terms for describing the shape of a member. For example, the sided dimension of a stem is an indication of its thickness; its molded dimension is its width when viewed in profile.

Spile
To determine and scribe a line that defines the shape of any element in a hull, so it will exactly fit on adjoining element as required. Most frequently, to transfer the shape of the upper edge of a plank or strake onto the bottom edge of the plank to be fastened immediately above it.

Stem
The foremost vertical or nearly vertical structural member of a boat's hull, at the point where the two sides meet at the bow.

Stock
The unfinished material something is to be made from. Stock is usually wood or lumber in woodworking, but in metalworking it is metal.

Strake

A single unit of planking that runs from the bow to the stern. A strake can be made of several pieces joined end to end.

Tumblehome

The inward curve of the topsides of a hull toward the centerline. More commonly found in the after portion of the hull.

Waterline

Any horizontal line on a boat's profile generated by a plane parallel to the surface of the water. The load waterline is the upper limit of a boat's draft under normal conditions with the designed load.

NOTES

NOTES

Boatbuilding Books from

How to Build the Shellback Dinghy
by Eric Dow

  Construct a beautiful dinghy following the step-by-step instructions of builder Eric Dow. The Shellback Dinghy is a modern classic with a traditional bow, a narrow rockered bottom, and a sweet transom that lifts well out of the water. Engineered with the amateur builder in mind, the Shellback has a practically frameless interior (there's a single laminated 'midship frame), which also makes her easy to clean and paint. The glued-lapstrake construction means she won't dry out when stored out of water for long periods of time.
Product #325-040
64 pp., illus., softcover
$15.00

How to Build the Haven 12 ½-Footer
by Maynard Bray

  Developed by Joel White for a client who loved the Herreshoff 12½ but required a shallow draft, the Haven 12½ is a keel/centerboard variation of the original. This book will show you how to construct her using the same process used to build the original Herreshoffs in Bristol, Rhode Island. She's built upside down, with a mold for every frame. No lofting is required. Each step in this unique process is carefully explained and illustrated, which, with detailed construction plans (not included), provides a thorough guide for advanced amateurs.
Product #325-077
64 pp., illus., softcover
$15.00

Building the Nutshell Pram
by Maynard Bray

  A step-by-step manual for the construction of this very popular Joel White design, for oar and sail. This revised instruction book is beneficial for anyone who wishes to build the pram from scratch using WoodenBoat's full-scale plans. Includes a listing of tools, materials, and fastenings, and more than 100 step-by-step photographs. Describes setting up, building, and fitting out the hull; constructing and installing the daggerboard trunk; making the rudder; rigging the pram for sail; and sailing techniques.
Product #325-035
32 pp., illus., softcover
$7.95

How to Build the Catspaw Dinghy:
A Boat for Oar and Sail
by the Editors of WoodenBoat

  A detailed manual on the building of a superior rowing and sailing dinghy. A modified version of the famous Herreshoff Columbia model dinghy, this boat, which measures 12' 8", makes an excellent project for the boatbuilder with intermediate skills. It is fitted with a centerboard and a simple sprit rig, and is built carvel style over steam-bent frames. The boat can be built right out of this guide (although using the plans is recommended), which contains carefully illustrated step-by-step building instructions, and reduced lines, offsets, construction plan, and sail plan.
Product #325-010
32 pp., illus., softcover
$8.95

WoodenBoat Publications

Forty Wooden Boats
by the Editors of WoodenBoat

Our study plans catalogs are best-sellers because they allow you to compare and contrast a variety of designs and building techniques along with providing vital statistics. Information includes beam, length, sail area, suggested engine, alternative construction methods, skill level needed (ranked by beginner, intermediate or advanced builder), level of detail provided in each plan, plus thought-provoking commentary.

Some of the 40 designs include L. Francis Herreshoff's ROZINANTE, Brewer's Mystic Sharpie, 5 kayaks built in a variety of methods (including a double-kayak), a canoe, 2 peapods (one of traditional plank-on-frame construction, the other glued-lap plywood), a catamaran, daysailers, a single and double rowing shell, skiffs, mahogany runabouts from the boards of Nelson Zimmer and Ken Bassett, and many more. The reader will find a tremendous amount of information at their fingertips at a very low price. These are the newest designs added to WoodenBoat's collection since the publication of *Fifty Wooden Boats* and *Thirty Wooden Boats*.
Product #325-062
96 pp., illus., softcover
$12.95

Fifty Wooden Boats
by the Editors of WoodenBoat

This popular book contains details usually found with study plans: hull dimensions, displacement, sail area, construction methods, and the degree of boatbuilding skill needed to complete each project. Along with the 50 designs—which range from a 7' 7" pram to a 41'3" schooner— there are drawings that identify the parts of a wooden boat, a bibliography, a guide for the selection of various woods, and instructions by Weston Farmer on reading boat plans. Unlike most plans catalogs, *Fifty Wooden Boats* also contains lines that let you see the hulls' shapes.
Product #325-060
112 pp., illus., softcover
$12.95

Thirty Wooden Boats
by the Editors of WoodenBoat

More study plans selected by the Editors of *WoodenBoat*. This volume describes the designs that were added to our collection after the publication of *Fifty Wooden Boats*.

These 30 designs include: 6 powerboats, 6 daysailers, 11 cruising boats, 2 canoes, a kayak, and 4 small sailing/pulling boats. Also included is an article by designer Joel White on understanding boat plans.
Product #325-061
80 pp., illus., softcover
$12.95

The WoodenBoat Store
P.O. Box 78 • Brooklin, ME 04616-0078
Call Toll-Free U.S. & Canada: 1–800–273–SHIP (7447)

The WoodenBoat Store

P.O. Box 78, Naskeag Road, Brooklin, Maine 04616-0078

EMail: wbstore@woodenboat.com

Toll-Free U.S. & Canada:
1-800-273-SHIP (7447)

Hours: 8am–6pm EST, Mon.–Fri. (9–5 Sats. Oct.–Dec.)
24-Hour Fax: 207-359-8920 **Overseas:** Call 207-359-4647
Internet Address: http://www.woodenboat.com

Ordered by _____

Address _____

_____

City/State/Zip _____

Day Phone# _____

| Catalog Code | **WPB** |

SHIP TO — only if different than "ORDERED BY"

Name _____

Address _____

_____

City/State/Zip _____

Product #	Qty.	Item, Size, Color	Ship Wt.	Total

WoodenBoat Magazine—US Subscriptions: One-year $27.00, Two-years $51.00, Three-years $75.00

SUB TOTAL	
Maine Residents Add 6% Tax	
❏ Standard / ❏ Priority Mail	
❏ Two Day / ❏ Next Day	
❏ Int'l Surface / ❏ Int'l Air	
TOTAL	

Our Guarantee... Satisfaction or Your Money Back!

Pre-payment is required. Payment MUST be in U.S. funds payable on a U.S. bank,

VISA **VISA** MasterCard **MasterCard** Discover **DISCOVER** Check, or Money Orders.

CARD NUMBER		EXPIRES Month/Year (required)
SIGNATURE OF CARDHOLDER		

U.S. Shipping Charges

	Standard Delivery		Priority Mail		Rush Delivery	
Zip Codes up to 49999		50000+	49999	50000	Two Day	Next Day
Minimum	$2.00	$2.00	$3.00	$3.00	$7.50	$12.00
½ to 1 lb.	3.00	3.00	3.00	3.00	7.50	13.50
up to 2 lbs.	3.00	3.00	3.00	3.00	8.50	14.50
up to 5 lbs.	4.50	6.00	6.50	6.50	9.50	18.50
up to 10 lbs	5.00	8.00	10.00	14.50	15.50	26.00
up to 15 lbs	6.00	10.00	14.00	20.00	21.50	31.50
Add for each additional 5 lbs.	+1.00	+2.00	+5.00	+5.00	+5.00	+5.00

Alaska and Hawaii ADD $10.00 to Two Day and Next Day Charges (No PO Boxes.)

International Shipping

CANADIAN CHARGES	OVERSEAS SURFACE	OVERSEAS PRIORITY/AIR
Up to1/2 lb. $3.00	Up to 1/2 lb.$4.00	Up to 1/2 lb.$7.00
Up to 2 lbs. 5.00	Up to 2 lbs. 9.00	Up to 1 lbs. 13.00
Up to 3 lbs. 6.50	Up to 3 lbs. 11.00	Up to 2 lbs. 22.00
Up to 4 lbs. 8.00	Up to 4 lbs. 13.00	Up to 3 lbs. 28.00
		Up to 4 lbs. 34.00
ADD $1.50 for each additional lb. PRIORITY/AIR: ADD $2.00 to Total	ADD $2.00 for each additional lb. (Allow 2-4 months for delivery)	ADD $6.00 for each additional lb. (Allow 2-4 weeks)

The WoodenBoat Store

P.O. Box 78, Naskeag Road, Brooklin, Maine 04616-0078

EMail: wbstore@woodenboat.com

Toll-Free U.S. & Canada:
1-800-273-SHIP (7447)

Hours: 8am–6pm EST, Mon.–Fri. (9–5 Sats. Oct.–Dec.)
24-Hour Fax: 207-359-8920 **Overseas:** Call 207-359-4647
Internet Address: http://www.woodenboat.com

Ordered by _____

Address _____

_____

City/State/Zip _____

Day Phone# _____

Catalog Code **WPB**

SHIP TO — only if different than "ORDERED BY"

Name _____

Address _____

_____

City/State/Zip _____

Product #	Qty.	Item, Size, Color	Ship Wt.	Total

WoodenBoat Magazine—US Subscriptions: One-year $27.00, Two-years $51.00, Three-years $75.00

Our Guarantee... Satisfaction or Your Money Back!

Pre-payment is required. Payment MUST be in U.S. funds payable on a U.S. bank,
VISA **VISA**   MasterCard **MasterCard**   Discover **DISCOVER**   Check, or Money Orders.

SUB TOTAL	
Maine Residents Add 6% Tax	
❏ Standard ❏ Priority Mail	
❏ Two Day ❏ Next Day	
❏ Int'l Surface ❏ Int'l Air	
TOTAL	

CARD NUMBER

SIGNATURE OF CARDHOLDER

EXPIRES Month/Year (required)

U.S. Shipping Charges

	Standard Delivery		Priority Mail		Rush Delivery	
Zip Codes up to 49999	50000+		49999	50000	Two Day	Next Day
Minimum	$2.00	$2.00	$3.00	$3.00	$7.50	$12.00
½ to 1 lb.	3.00	3.00	3.00	3.00	7.50	13.50
up to 2 lbs.	3.00	3.00	3.00	3.00	8.50	14.50
up to 5 lbs.	4.50	6.00	6.50	6.50	9.50	18.50
up to 10 lbs	5.00	8.00	10.00	14.50	15.50	26.00
up to 15 lbs	6.00	10.00	14.00	20.00	21.50	31.50
Add for each additional 5 lbs.	+1.00	+2.00	+5.00	+5.00	+5.00	+5.00

Alaska and Hawaii ADD $10.00 to Two Day and Next Day Charges (No PO Boxes.)

International Shipping

CANADIAN CHARGES	OVERSEAS SURFACE	OVERSEAS PRIORITY/AIR
Up to 1/2 lb. $3.00	Up to 1/2 lb.$4.00	Up to 1/2 lb.$7.00
Up to 2 lbs. 5.00	Up to 2 lbs. 9.00	Up to 1 lbs. 13.00
Up to 3 lbs. 6.50	Up to 3 lbs. 11.00	Up to 2 lbs. 22.00
Up to 4 lbs. 8.00	Up to 4 lbs. 13.00	Up to 3 lbs. 28.00
		Up to 4 lbs. 34.00
ADD $1.50 for each additional lb. PRIORITY/AIR: ADD $2.00 to Total	ADD $2.00 for each additional lb. (Allow 2-4 months for delivery)	ADD $6.00 for each additional lb. (Allow 2-4 weeks)